Conversation Marketing

A Facebook Tactical Guide

Written by Clifford VanMeter
Chief Marketing Technologist
Arctos Media, Inc.

Edited By Caitlin VanMeter

Table of Contents

Introduction 3

Why Content Marketing is Dead.................................... 11

Social Influence 18

Your Facebook Journey 21

What is Social Selling 25

How the Facebook News Feed Works 31

Where? What? When? 40

The Social Media Audit 43

Building Your Facebook Brand 49

Reviews & Testimonials 64

Responding 67

Facebook Messenger 74

Going Prospecting 80

Facebook Advertising Platform 87

Creating Facebook Ad Campaigns 96

Building Ads 110

Using Videos 133

Analytics 146

Understanding Your Facebook Audiences 167

In Conclusion 182

Online & Dealership Acronyms 184

Introduction

Here's a fun fact: the age of *interruption marketing* is over. Fini. Kaput. As dead as a doornail.

TV, radio, even print advertising were always about getting your message between the prospective customer and the content they wanted, then hoping they'd be more interested than angry. Sure, if you were good enough; if your content was compelling enough; or if you happened to hit them at just the right time, you had a chance to make a connection, but like the man said, "We know half our advertising budget is wasted, we just don't know which half.[1]"

In the last few years, the shift from interruption marketing to **content marketing** has largely been driven by online advertising options and Google's algorithm updates. The pursuit of Search Engine Optimization (*SEO*) is all about looking for the secret sauce in content marketing these days. What Google has done is refine their technology to ensure that

---

[1] Attributed to John Wanamaker

their users see only the most relevant, important, and useful information with every search.

Gone are the days when you could game the system by buying links, stuffing landing pages with irrelevant keywords and generally trying to deceive your way to traffic. Now content must be relevant to make its mark.

Content Marketing is about embracing these realities. It's about accepting that there is a right way and a wrong way to engage your customers and potential customers. There are rules laid down by Google and other search engines that ensure your customers will only find you if you are providing something of value to them.

This is where content marketing really begins to make an impact. Content marketing, done correctly (using purely white-hat techniques) will drive traffic to your site by ensuring that you have relevant information for the user. It's that word relevant that's most important. Relevant info, delivered to a relevant audience, at the relevant time.

> *Remember this: It's better to talk to 100 people who care about your message, than 100,000 who don't.*

That's what content marketing is trying to be about; identifying your audience, identifying their interests, and supplying valuable content centered on those interests.

A lot has been said and written in the last couple of years about content marketing and content marketing is moving in the right direction, but it doesn't go far enough on its own. We need to get a step further down the road and focus on *conversation marketing*. This is where social media, especially Facebook comes into play.

To properly use social media as a viable lead producing source, we have to shift our focus from yelling into the darkness hoping someone will hear, to engaging people directly. Social Media and Facebook in particular give us the opportunity to engage people in several ways. One-to-one marketing. Personalized conversations will inevitably lead to conversions.

An industry leader in sales and marketing technology refers to the shift to customer-centric sales and marketing as *Inbound*, but inbound, like content marketing, is just a subset of what I've chosen to call *Conversation Marketing*.

Conversation marketing has a broader focus than either inbound or content marketing alone. It's about *touches*. It's like tapping someone on the shoulder and saying, "Excuse me, I couldn't help but overhear that you have a problem with X. I've found that solution Y is a good approach to solving that problem." It's about getting their attention and focusing your attention on giving them something of value. That's the new marketing, not talking people into solutions they don't need, they already have too many resources that they can bring to bear to call BS on artificially inflated claims. You need to provide real value over time and build a relationship based on trust with the customer. As Zig Ziglar said, "If people like you they'll listen to you, but if they trust you they'll do business with you."

As I'll show you later on in the book, liking is easy. Trust must be earned, and that takes time. Conversation Marketing can be useful for call-to-action marketing, but where it really shines is in taking the longer view. Building a network of relationships that will feed you sales and referrals.

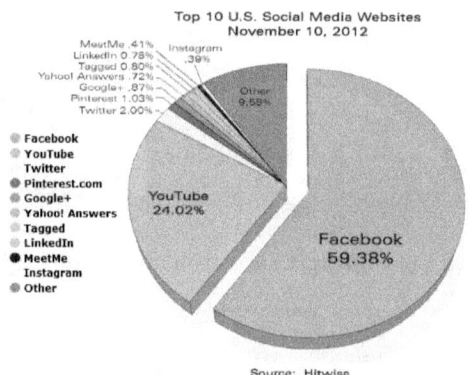

Top 10 U.S. Social Media Websites
November 10, 2012

MeetMe .41%
LinkedIn 0.78%
Tagged 0.80%
Yahoo! Answers .72%
Google+ .87%
Pinterest 1.03%
Twitter 2.00%
Instagram .39%
Other 9.59%

Facebook
YouTube
Twitter
Pinterest.com
Google+
Yahoo! Answers
Tagged
LinkedIn
MeetMe
Instagram
Other

YouTube 24.02%

Facebook 59.38%

Source: Hitwise

So in light of the broadness that I claim conversation marketing has, why have I chosen to focus so narrowly on Facebook? To say that Facebook is the number one social media site simply doesn't give you a sense of just how massive Facebook is by comparison. This particular chart is from 2012, and it shows Facebook at 60% of ALL social media interactions. YouTube plays a strong second. I'll admit a few things have changed in that time.

YouTube now accounts for a smaller percentage thanks to Facebook's emphasis on native video. Add that to Facebook's purchase and integration of Instagram, and Facebook is now at closer to **80%** of all social media engagement.

Let that sink in for a minute. LinkedIn, Twitter, Vine, Pinterest, etc. account for just about 20% of all social media interactions. So assuming you have limited resources (like time and money), you want to focus your energies where you'll get the best and most immediate response. That's Facebook.

There are so many strategic options for advertising and for organic reach, that I felt the need to create a walk-through, a tactical guide. Sure there are thousands of articles, videos and tutorials out there that will give you a great strategic overview, or that focus on one specific aspect or another,

but a tactical, workflow-driven approach is what's needed and what's been sorely lacking. Blogs and websites tend to be more strategic than tactical.

Another problem with social media strategies is that people tend to treat the different aspects of Facebook (such as paid posts, lead generation, and organic reach) as though they were discrete elements instead of what they really are; cogs in a single machine. It's only when we combine all these different aspects of promotion and prospecting that we achieve optimal results.

You have to think of online marketing like a watch. Facebook is one gear in that watch. So are phone calls, emails, direct mails, data mining, and websites. They work great in concert, but start taking away one or another and the watch stops.

If you approach Facebook advertising and marketing from this point of view, and follow the step-by-step plans laid out in this book, you will achieve the generation of more leads, more conversions, and more sold customers.

How much more? One client I have, the place I started and worked to refine these techniques, saw a 400% increase in leads generated. In fact, in a recent managers' meeting one manager requested that we shrink his geographic zone to generate fewer leads because his staff could keep up with the volume of leads being handed to them.

As one of my old bosses used to say, "These are the problems we *want* to have."

Why Content Marketing (Alone) is Already (Mostly) Dead

Bill Gates famously said, "Content is king!"

If you've been involved in online marketing for any period of time, you've heard this. The idea of *Content Marketing* really started to take hold after Google's last few algorithm updates. In particular Panda, Penguin and the Hummingbird updates to the core search algorithm.

I won't go into the technical details of these changes, but the fact that the Penguin Update was referred to by marketers as the *Peguipocolypse* should give you some idea of their profound affect.

Penguin was a game changer for a lot of what I call *shortcut marketers*. These are the marketers that were always looking for a way to game the system. Link farms, paid reviews, etc. They all wanted the short cut to SEO. Some magic formula that would solve all their problems.

I'm here to tell you my friend; there is no shortcut to mastering your online presence, whether you're a brand or an individual salesman. There is a formula to make it easier, even automate parts of the process, but this is no shortcut. The difference

Google wants you to produce content that is relevant to its users and it rewards you by delivering you more traffic through its search engine results. That seems simple enough. Create content that people want, and get in front of more people without having to spend a fortune on advertising.

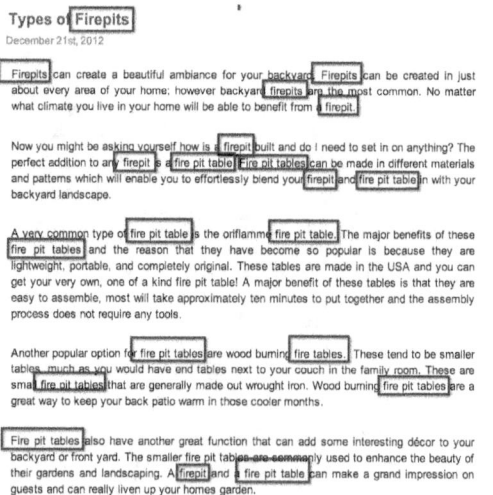

The problem for most businesses isn't grasping the underlying concepts, but the execution. More than 90% of customers WANT more content from the brands they follow, but only 10% of customers think these brands do it well.

Too many times content is simply thrown together, stuffed with keywords, and pushed out through a company blog or by press releases and news aggregators.

Branding or *top of mind awareness* helps your business become identifiable to your market. It establishes who you are in the minds of the prospective buyer. The real problem is that it doesn't go far enough. It's the long game, and we do need the long game, but we also need the short game; *Call-to-action marketing.*

Automotive marketers in particular have always struggled with call-to-action marketing. Starbucks runs a sale or introduces a new latte and there is an instant response from the public. That's because coffee drinkers drink coffee daily. They have a built-in sense of urgency.

McDonald's shamrock shakes are another great example of what I call *automatic urgency.* You know you can only get them in March, so you are driven by the scarcity to get in there and get it quick. Even if you wouldn't be caught dead buying anything else at McDonald's, you show up to get the Shamrock Shakes.

Compare that to an auto buyer. Auto buyers often have very little sense of urgency. Statistically we're looking at car buyers purchasing a new vehicle every 3-5 years. They often believe they can get through one more month or one more winter with that old car. In fact, only about 2% of your audience are what I call *active buyers.*

Over 90% of households will order pizza this month, but just 2% are interested in buying a new vehicle. It's time to either get into the pizza business, or accept the reality that you need to work on the other 98%. You can either nudge them further down the sales funnel, or at the very least be there when they are in the market and ready to buy.

Of the two, the best option is to nudge and nurture. Give them the gentle push needed to move them to the Active Buyer stage (the people looking to buy within the next four weeks). What are sometimes also referred to as *buyer intenders*, or Tier 3 Prospects.

I call that 98%, *inactive buyers*. Why call them buyers at all? Because practically every household in America has a car, truck minivan or SUV. Sooner or later, they will buy, but you have an immediate need to produce results. Call-to-action marketing and *Conversation Marketing* used together to create buyer context, can and do drive buyers who are in the market now and encourage inactive buyers to make the jump. What, how soon and from whom will they buy are the critical questions that you need to supply the answer for.

When looking at my version of the traditional sales funnel I break prospects into the three categories pictured on the next page.

Browsers

People looking, but who
have not yet decided to
buy. They lack
decisiveness.

Lookers

Potential customers who
have made the decision to
buy, but have not yet
decided when or where.
They lack urgency.

Buyers

These are the low-hanging
fruit. Those people who
have made a decision to
buy and are looking to buy
now. They only lack a
compelling reason to buy
from you, rather than your
competitor.

In addition to being converted to active buyers, inactive buyers can be
recruited to act as Brand Advocates; the proverbial friend-of-a-friend
who promotes your product or service. They might not be in the market

right now, but they may be willing to recommend you. Making them brand advocates is also a great nurturing step in making them customers later on.

Each social media platform provides a different kind of connection. Facebook is your number one resource for conversation marketing because it's more than 80% of daily social interactions.

As we start to look at the specifics, we understand the context and you'll begin to understand that there are millions of conversations taking place round the clock on Facebook. It's as simple as joining the conversation by finding people who are anxious to listen to what you have to say.

Social Influence

On the whole social media is about making and maintaining connections with customers and potential customers. In Robert Cialdini's great book, *Influence*, he defines what he calls the six pillars of influence. We could just as easily call these the six pillars of sales and marketing. These are:

- Reciprocity — Give something to get something back;
- Scarcity — The harder it is to get, the more people want it;
- Authority — We trust those who demonstrate their authority;
- Liking — We buy from people we like;
- Consistency — Small agreements lead to larger agreements;
- Consensus — We look to the opinions of others to support our decisions.

I firmly believe the most important of those pillars is *Liking*. People do business with people they like; this is been true throughout the entire existence of the human race.

How do you get someone to like you? It's really quite simple. Find something you have in common. For example: You're on the phone with a prospect, and in the background you hear a dog bark. You can tell it's a small dog from the sound of the bark. So you ask the prospect," What kind of dog do you have? Really, my dog is a..." Right there you've established an area of commonality. They have a dog. You have a dog. You both have dogs. You've gotten them to like you in 5-seconds flat.

On Facebook we literally have a *Like* button for people to show how much they like us. More than that, we get people to like us by sharing about ourselves and letting people get to know us.

With the possible exception of scarcity, Facebook strikes every single note of the pillars of influence when it's used properly.

- Reciprocity. If the posts you share have a value to people; they are entertaining, amusing or educational in some way that is important to them — people will be more receptive to your prospecting approaches.
- Authority and Consensus are supported by your number of friends and the number of shares and likes on your posts.
- Consistency comes into play when someone says they are looking for a solution and you provide one.

So, as you can see, providing quality posts, on a regular basis is what separates the casual marketer from the professional marketer on Facebook.

Your Facebook Journey

To begin we need to take stock of where we are. After all, you can't map a strategy to move forward if you don't know where you're starting from.

In most cases, you're going to be in one of these stages of Facebook adoption within your organization:

> **Traditional**: You're right at the beginning. You might have dipped your toe into the Facebook pond, you probably have a profile, but no Facebook page, or if you do have one it's not regularly updated (which is actually worse than not having one).

> **Experimental**: You're getting there, taking your first tentative steps into posting, commenting, you might even have joined a group or two. You're either running very few Facebook ads, or none at all. Any you are running are more likely to be boosted posts than the more sophisticated offers like Leads Ads.

> **Operational**: You have a fully developed Facebook content strategy that includes regular posts to your own page with video and photos. You're regularly using boosted posts to drive like and engagement. You're also watching messenger

and responding to messages and comments. You'll also be checking your KPIs to ensure that your tactics are effective.

Impactful: You've got on your big-boy pants and you're doing everything above, but your running location promotions, offers, lead ads. You're also effectively using and monitoring all this and you've got a clear understanding of your Facebook ROI.

Your challenge now is to be as honest with yourself as possible and determine which stage of the process you are in. Everything else you determine using this book is going to be impacted by your starting point. Just like how, if you're driving to Cleveland the route you take is influenced by whether you start in Chicago or Cincinnati.

Once you've determined your stage in the journey, you need to develop a your own Facebook Tactical Plan. Now you hear the words Strategy and Tactics thrown around interchangeably a lot. They aren't the same thing. A Strategy is about visualizing the outcome you expect. Strategy should be as specific as possible to make it measurable, for example my strategy is to increase website traffic to increase overall lead generation.

Now you break down the steps to achieve the strategy. Those tactics are broken down into tasks with individual staff members assigned to implement those tasks and who are held accountable for that implementation. It breaks down as shown below:

1. Strategy: Increase website traffic and lead generation by 20%.
   a. Tactic 1: Use Facebook boosted posts with a *Shop Now* link to our inventory page.
      i. Schedule walk-around videos each week for our Facebook.
         1. Task 1: Sales staff are now required to produce one walk-around video each week and upload it to YouTube for syndication. Manager must report to GSM on who did and did not complete this task weekly.
         2. Task 2: Marketing department to set up YouTube Channel and provide login and password to all store managers.
         3. Task 3: Marketing department to caption and download videos, then upload them as Facebook native videos (with captions).

A full tactical plan for this strategy would include several tactics, with each tactic including many specific tasks assigned by department (as in this case) or to individuals. It's just far too easy for a step to fall through the cracks or be forgotten if there isn't a clear plan moving forward.

What is social selling?

Building a large following may at first appear to be the goal when it comes to social media marketing, but there's no point having a million followers if no-one is buying. To get the most out of your social media activity it's important to be more than just seen. What you really want is to encourage action. On the other hand, shoving sales messages down people's throats will not encourage them to stick around. So how can you use social media in general, and specifically Facebook, to convert connections into sales?

While you may already be using social media to get your company name, products and services out there, the buzzword of the moment is *social selling*, which is a far more tactical and integrated approach.

It's about generating revenue and putting strategies in place that are designed to make a sale. From a conversion point of view it needs to lead to the product, not come from the product.

Really think of it like this, there are two main strategies for generating leads. In my book *Social Selling* (ASIN: B01FZTQ2W0), I cover fishing with a spear or pole. Reeling in one prospect at a time. This is great for the individual salesman working social media on his own.

Conversation marketing is about fishing with a net, but unlike legacy marketing or interruption marketing, conversation marketing fishes only the most productive fishing holes so it produces the best results with the highest ROI.

To get started, begin by thinking through your sales process from start to finish and breaking down how social media could be used to best support each stage of the sales funnel.

As I mentioned earlier, most of us learned the three stage sales funnel. It's been around for years. I label the stages, Browsers, Lookers and Buyers. Facebook is an amazing tool to push or pull prospects from one level to the next, through the sales funnel.

Here are some strategies that we'll examine in greater detail later.

Potential Prospects: Worldwide, there are over 1.59 billion monthly active Facebook users. That's thousands or millions of potential customers out there, even on a local or regional level. They are there just waiting for you to find them. One of the best things about Facebook is that they have opened up incredible possibilities for you to not only find them, but target and connect with them. Facebook also operates in real-time, so you're right there at the right time to take full advantage of the needs of the prospective customer.

Start By Listening: Facebook has made it far easier to research and pull together data that can help tailor an approach to new customers, but with great power, comes great responsibility. You need to think about who your target customer is and make sure you are listening to them. They're telling you what their needs are… What their pain is. Use what you learn to take create an offer or a product that will take that pain away. That is the basis of all good sales. Identify a need and offer a solution.

What can you learn from their posts and updates that may help you with your sales process? There are likely to be keywords in their discussions that identify a potential prospect. You know your product or service, think about how you can make sure you're alerted to them.

Remember, conversation marketing is about creating relationships. That requires you to listen as well as speak. You have two ears and one mouth. Listen at least twice as much as you speak.

Creating Credibility: PT Barnum is reported to have said, *"It's all about sincerity... if you can fake that, you've got it made."*

Seriously, though, generating and sharing interesting, insightful content is a key part of social selling. This includes content that isn't necessarily seen as selling, although I'm of the opinion that everything is selling.

Things like recipes, or funny videos can help establish your brand by creating a feeling of *NICE* about you and your employees. As well as posting quality information from the company that customers will want to read. You know you need to start by creating a profile of your customers, but to really optimize your online presence; the sales teams' profiles should also match in their messaging, their style, the quality of content and their imagery?

It's important that they all present a strong, unified image of the company and what it stands for. All these issues can affect your credibility. A company is nothing is really just a collection of human beings, but on the internet it's often not perceived that way. Showing your expertise, positioning yourself as an expert and giving a good impression across profiles, pages, and groups is critical to building trust. Training is key to how you and your staff create your online personas and how you connect with your prospects and customers.

Your Competition: Don't forget, social media can also help you track of the competition. Under *Insights* on your Facebook page, you'll find *Pages to Watch*. This is a great way to monitor your competitor's' pages in comparison to your own.

Look at how often they post, how many likes they have and how quickly they are adding new ones. This will help inform your content calendar. Follow competitors and their employees to keep tabs on what they're talking about. You'll be surprised what you can pick up on.

Competition is good.

How the Facebook News Feed Works

Facebook has made significant changes to the news feed algorithm lately. These changes have a direct affect on who sees your posts.

Previously, Facebook wouldn't give higher organic reach to instant articles in the news feed. However, that didn't mean instant articles wouldn't be used to help determine what posts should get more organic reach. The image below is a simplified version of what I call the News Feed Equation. Facebook actually looks at roughly 100,000 other personalized factors when deciding what to show an individual user.

Facebook now uses time spent reading or watching content as the primary signal that a story or video was important to the user. The *time spent viewing* metric is now also used to predict what other content users will find interesting. Then Facebook shows users similar content.

This actually meshes with Hubspot's hyper-successful inbound sales philosophy perfectly, because it focuses on meeting the customer's (in this case the Facebook user's) needs first. Everything needs to be centered on what they want to know, not what you want to tell them. That's why you need to make sure you're focused on their needs, wants and desires and that everything you tell them in a selling more is phrasec in their context as benefits not features.

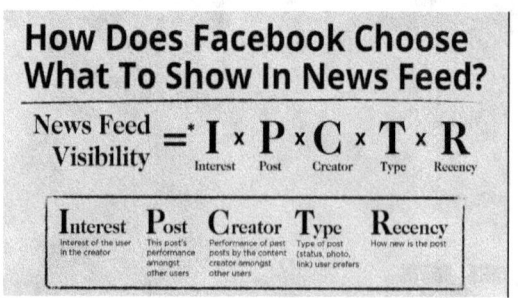

How Does Facebook Choose What To Show In News Feed?

$$\text{News Feed Visibility} =^* \underset{\text{Interest}}{I} \times \underset{\text{Post}}{P} \times \underset{\text{Creator}}{C} \times \underset{\text{Type}}{T} \times \underset{\text{Recency}}{R}$$

Interest	Post	Creator	Type	Recency
Interest of the user in the creator	This post's performance amongst other users	Performance of past posts by the content creator amongst other users	Type of post (status, photo, link) user prefers	How new is the post

If you want more your viewers to see more of your content in the news feed, make sure that you maximize their time spent viewing. Time spent viewing might seem like a hurdle, but there are ways you can maximize time spent viewing so your posts get optimal organic engagement.

1. Be sure that your content delivers what the headline promises. You need to craft a headline that's irresistible enough to click, and include a video or article introduction to show you'll deliver on that headline.

2. Create longer videos and articles, but not too long. Facebook looks at the time spent on a piece of content within a maximum threshold. Videos of 2-3 minutes, or articles of about 600 words are best.

Remember, the goal is to make sure viewers don't click into your content, then immediately click away.

In addition to time spent viewing, Facebook wants to add diversity to the news feed. Facebook has figured out that most users aren't just interested in one or two things, they have wide ranging interests and want their newsfeeds to reflect that. Users are also interested in seeing content from a wide-range of publishers. Not just back-to-back articles or videos from the same publishers.

This clearly works against brands that push too much content; since Facebook will reduce how often users see several posts in a row from the same source.

It can be tricky, but you can use this drive toward diversity to your advantage. One of the main ways to take advantage of this new initiative is to simply slow down. You probably don't need to be that company that publishes five or more posts per day. Most studies agree that twice per day is actually the magic number. Fewer and you're not taking full advantage of the platform, and more than twice a day actually see less engagement and now less organic reach.

Another way to be more diverse and still appear multiple times in the news feed is to repurpose content. I like repurposing content. Not only does it help amortize the cost of creating the content across multiple platforms, but now with this push for diversity, repurposing or republishing content across platforms can help ensure greater organic reach.

> For example, you could share multiple pieces of content per day from your blog, Facebook notes, a LinkedIn Pulse, or from different Facebook accounts like your page, your employee's profiles, or your Facebook groups.

Another important thing to remember about how the Facebook news feed works is that the feed algorithm updates it with Facebook's stated mission to connect users with the stories that matter most to them.

Ultimately, Facebook's news feed mission should be *your* mission. Each time you create content, you should be creating stories that matter to your target audience.

Connecting

As you connect with more people and like more pages, your news feed changes to show you more from those people and those pages. Even the groups you join play a role in what news feed content is seen.

A good place to start to increase your organic reach is to find out who loves your brand, your products, your services, and your content. Once you've identified the people who talk about you or share what you publish, recommend that people follow them. Make that person your featured fan of the week or the month. The individual will be happy to get new followers, and you'll be happy the next time he or she mentions you or shares your content.

You can also identify other businesses, and highlight them as someone you use or respect. Point out your relationship with vendors, trusted suppliers, and the like. Write them a review and/or post a thank you on their page. Mention them, or hashtag (#) them in a post on your page. The businesses will be happy to get new fans, and it will benefit you when they mention you or share your content.

Facebook also takes several factors into account when deciding how to prioritize a post. Including the type of content shared: text, photo, video, or a link. If users typically engage with photos more than videos, they'll likely be shown more photos than videos. In general photos get about 5x the level of engagement as text status updates, and videos get 15x the level of engagement as text.

Now that statistic can be misleading. Clearly video has the highest organic reach, but not everyone likes video. It's important to diversify your content; post one text-only update, one photo update, one video update (directly uploaded to Facebook with captions), and one link. This will ensure that you've created at least one post with a content type that appeals to all of your fans.

Another couple of factors that Facebook uses when deciding a post's priority is engagement and recency. This is why consistent posting is so important. If you haven't posted anything in days or weeks, chances are nothing from you is going to show up in your audience's news feed.

Even if you are posting every day, when someone else posts something that has more engagement, chances are the user will see the post with more interactions first, even though your post is more recent.

So recency and interactions go hand in hand. Make sure you post often so you always have posts for Facebook to consider showing to your fans. You also want to make sure that your posts are getting the maximum engagement possible.

For special posts you want to make sure everyone sees, focus on getting maximum engagement and make sure you give that post an extra bump through Facebook advertising or even just sharing a direct link to the Facebook post to other social media audiences.

Even as I'm writing this, Facebook continues to make changes to how the news feed algorithm works. A good start would be to follow the News Feed FYI :

http://newsroom.fb.com/news/category/news-feed-fyi/.

This will keep you abreast of changes to the Facebook news feed algorithm. Also follow the Facebook Media Blog (https://media.fb.com/blog/) for tips on how you can get more out of Facebook and to prepare for upcoming changes.

Here are a few general tips to keep in mind that will help you take better advantage of your Facebook presence:

- Write compelling headlines, not click-bait. You know what I mean, "Here are 10 Amazing things. You'll never believe number 8." These kinds of headlines often disappoint. Try to write headlines that actually let the user know what to expect and they are more likely to spend time reading your article or watching your video.

- Remember the Rule of Five. One selling post for every five posts total. Too much pushy, preachy, salesmany content will lose you followers. Be interesting. Be funny. Be entertaining. Then when you go to push your product or program they'll allow you to be heard.

- Experiment. What's best for one audience is not best for another. Try short form, long form, video, and different tones. Then use Publisher Tools and Insights to see what actually works.

- Use Audience Optimization. It will allow you to specify audiences that will be interested in your content. Facebook will use it as part of the ranking in particular users' news feeds.

Where? What? When?

So we've covered the where and the what, let's take a look at the when.

Facebook's internal audits have shown that the best time to post for maximum engagement is between 13:00 and 16:00 (that's 1PM-4PM for you civilians) during the week, with Wednesday as the peak day.

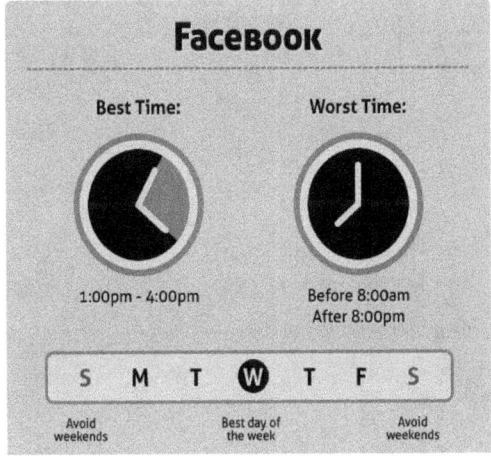

Weekends are bad for engagement overall, so you should avoid posting on Saturdays and Sundays. Also avoid posting before 8AM and after 8PM, as these times show a sharp drop off in engagement.

Once you've answered when, you're left with the question of how often.
The answer is a simple one.

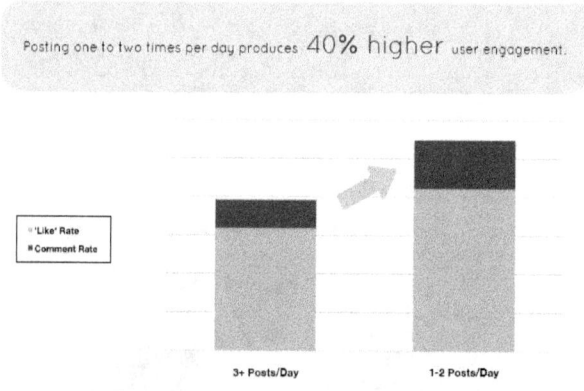

Posting one to two times per day produces 40% higher user engagement.

- Brands that post less than once per day get 40% less
  engagement than brands who do.
- Brands that post more than twice a day get 20% less
  engagement.

That's right, posting too much is almost as bad as not posting enough.
So twice a day in the afternoon is the best option. If you want to be a
little fancier, try posting once on Mondays and Fridays, twice on Tues-
Thursdays, and lay off entirely on the weekends.

The Social Media Audit

Before you start really using Facebook as a company marketing tool, you need to prepare. The first step is to find out what you have, and where it is on Facebook. For example; how many of your employees already have profiles? Pages? Are there groups or pages set up previously and abandoned? Are employees maintaining their own active pages? Are there negative groups or pages (like Cliff's Auto Sales Sucks)?

Next determine how active these pages or groups are. One of my clients had a *SUCKS* page set up about them. We could put a lot of effort into challenging the page on trademark grounds, or going after the page owner in various ways, but the fact is after 6-months they have about 12 fans. So the best thing to do is leave them alone. If, on the other hand, there were 120 or even 1200 fans the first approach would be to reach out to the page admin and find out if there's a way to make things right with them, then get them to delete the page. Only as an absolute last resort should you go after them through Facebook, or through legal means like a cease and desist letter.

A word about the Streisand Effect: The Streisand effect is the phenomenon where attempts to hide, remove, or censor a piece of information has the unintended consequence of publicizing the information more widely.

It's named after Barbra Streisand, whose attempt to suppress photo-graphs of her residence in Malibu, California, inadvertently drew further public attention to it. Similar attempts have been made in cease-and-desist letters to suppress numbers, files, or websites. Instead of being suppressed, they receive extensive publicity and media extensions such as videos and spoof songs, often being widely mirrored across the Internet and on file-sharing networks.

Want to avoid getting caught by the Streisand Effect? It's often just a matter of listening to the customer and finding out what went wrong. A lot of times they just need to vent and hear you say, "I'm sorry."

Here's a link to an article about a dealership in my hometown of Kalamazoo, MI who completely mishandled as bad situation. As a result, he's caught right in the middle of the Streisand Effect. http://buff.ly/1UkqLL3/. If you aren't interested in looking it up, here's the basic idea. A woman purchased a car and left a bad review. She said the car's price was off and she felt cheated and deceived by staff. On the dealership's end, they deny everything. Some of this may sound like complaints you see every so often at your business. When the customer went to get what she paid to get her car repaired refunded, the company told her, "Remove your negative review and we will refund the warrantied amount." As you can imagine, things only escalated from there.

Here's the real point with negative pages or groups; People have a hard time staying angry in the long term. They might take the few minutes to set up the page or group, but they can't maintain that level of anger over the long term so they quickly abandon actually keeping it active.

As far as employee groups or pages, these can be helpful or hurtful; and sometimes the same page can be both. The important thing here is to make sure they fairly and accurately represent your brand. If they are and are willing to continue, AND they are active, then there is no reason not to let them continue to act as Brand Advocates. The key is that they must be consistent with your brand message and active. One more abandoned page does not help you.

Another thing to consider is your physical presence in the world. For example, do you have one rooftop or several? How far apart are they spaced? One of my clients is a dealer group with six rooftops spaced out from thirty minutes to more than two hours apart. We know from surveying their customer data that 85% of customers come from within 22 miles of their locations, so the focus needs to be more local than company-wide. For this kind of real world presence, they need to have separate pages for each rooftop. While this might, at first, seem like a lot of extra work, it's well worth it. You will be able to target more directly that local audience.

Also, Facebook itself wants you to lay out pages in such a way as to prefer individual listings, when you have brick and mortar locations. We'll look at how to manage multiple pages with automated online software like Buffer (http://bufferapp.com) a little later in this book.

Once you've completed the audit for yourself, I highly recommend you do it for your competitors as well. Knowing where they are and what they are up to should help inform your targets for how often, and what kind of content to post. Watch their engagement, and see what kinds of things they are successful with. If their customer profiles actually match yours (they are real competitors), you'll get a lot of good intelligence by watching what they are doing. Facebook can actually help you with that by using the *Pages To Watch* function, which we mentioned earlier.

Building Your Facebook Brand

Your presence on Facebook is made up of multiple pieces that should be treated as integrally linked. In other words, if Facebook is an engine, the different parts of your Facebook presence (including pages, profiles, groups, reviews, events, and offers) are all the components of that engine. None of these things exists in a vacuum and each of them can affect the others.

Your Facebook Page is central to your brand. Creating a Facebook Page for your company is the first basic step in becoming discoverable on Facebook. More than that, Facebook pages are indexed by search engines in much the same way that web pages are. For this reason, you must approach building your Facebook page(s) in much the same way you would with regard to optimizing your title, description and content for Google.

To begin with you need to understand the keywords that affect your search engine optimization. There's no way around it: without objective data, keyword research is a shot in the dark. Fortunately, Google has supplied us with a great free tool that tells you almost all of the information you need to make informed decisions about which keywords are best. It's called the Google Keyword Planner.

The new tool has an entire suite of features that will help you identify a keyword's growing (or shrinking) popularity, filter out low-volume searches, and create hundreds of keyword combinations in just seconds.

For our purposes here, we don't need hundreds of keywords. We only need to generate your top 10 keywords and key phrases.

Keep in mind that the tool is designed with Adwords advertisers in mind. So there are a lot of features in the tool like keyword bidding that won't be useful for this exercise.

Since an in depth session on Google's keyword research tool is beyond the scope of this book (and probably deserves its own book at some point), here is a link to a great video that gives you more detail. http://bit.ly/1FpKzJA

Name a Thing to Own It

When choosing your page's name, the obvious choice is to use your business name, but not all business names make it obvious what your industry or niche is. So adding a keyword to your page name can be a big help in that regard.

- Your page title should include one keyword;
- Your short description should include two;
- Your long description can include up to five.

Don't get too spammy with keywords, and make sure your descriptions don't start sounding artificial. For example, here's a well know example of a keyword stuffed posting from the internet. It's a great example of a really bad technique.

> *White* is a word on a *white* web page that is *white* because the background is *white*. *White* is a color. *White* is not black. *White* is lighter than green. There is also bright *white*, dark *white*, off *white*, etc, etc.

See how forced that sounds. Try to aim for something that still sounds like you're a real person talking to real people. Google, Facebook, and other such sites are aware of these keyword stuffing techniques and will actively punish you for using them. How do they punish you? They reduce your frequency in the search returns, or hide you all together.

Also, it's important to note that the first 18 characters of your description will be what Google grabs as part of your search returns. Make sure you take full advantage of those 18 characters by including your brand name at the beginning of the paragraph.

You can also embed keywords in your posts themselves. This helps optimize both for Facebook's internal search, and Google searches.

Another great way to add some link love is to put your website address at the end of each post. This way, when someone shares your post, they are also sharing your web address. This can help drive more traffic to your site. Even better than a home page link, is to use various links to landing pages with contact information, apply now, request a trade in quote, even profiles of your salespeople.

For video posts, Facebook now allows you to add a call-to-action button to the end of your video. These buttons are perfect for generating clicks to your website. I typically recommend using the "learn more," and "Shop Now," buttons.

In short, you should treat your Facebook page as if it's a mini-website all on it's own. Remember, it's even more than that; it is a community building tool. It is the conversational hub that allows you to connect with both current customers and prospects. It amplifies your conversations and allows you to reach large groups. It also gives you deeper insights into your audience. Once you have your page built, you should invite your contacts, friends and fans to like the page.

Once you've passed 25 likes, you'll be able to use the custom domain feature of your page and change from something like Facebook.com/69042h to something more like Facebook.com/cliffsauto. Not only is there an obvious branding improvement, but you become instantly more recognizable and memorable as well.

You'll also need to pass 50 likes before you can start boosted posts, one of the easiest to use advertising features on Facebook.

Visually Building Your Page

The appearance of your page needs to mirror your overall branding. Facebook only gives you limited graphical opportunities to customize your page, so you need to take full advantage of these.

- **Cover Photo**: This image sits at the top of your company profile page and rests behind your logo as a backdrop. The cover photo lends itself to creativity and should be changed frequently. It's the largest graphic on your page, and that real estate can be used to include a picture of your physical location, your staff, or even a non-related image that's fun, or interesting or just pretty. Be creative. Think of your cover photo, not just in literal terms of your brand, but in terms of what you'd like your viewers to feel when they first see it. Your cover photo could include brand messaging, campaign promotions, or product images—the potential choices are endless.

- **Profile Photo**: This image sits on the bottom left of your cover photo and is the icon by which you are identified all across Facebook. On your page it's slightly larger, but it also appears as small thumbnail that's attached to almost any action that you will take anywhere on Facebook —from posting in a group, to posting on your own timeline—this image represents you. For that reason it should be clear as to what it represents, even at its smallest size. Most companies will use a logo, or other branding element. Because of it's small size it's important to choose an easily identifiable image that includes little or no text. Your profile picture, like your actual logo, should rarely change.

- **About**: The about section is a *tab* in the navigation bar that lives under your profile photo and cover photo. *About* includes two sections. The first is your page information, This is your spot to share details about your company. This section includes a description, your awards, products, and contact information. The second element is milestones, which lets you commemorate and share important events in the history of your brand; when your company was founded, for example.

- **Timeline**: The core of your page, and the one section that will draw the most eyeballs is the Timeline. Think of this like a newsfeed, like those old-fashioned scrolling news tickers. Posting on Facebook is a key way to build followers and fuel your paid advertising efforts. These posts can be comprised of text, images, links, non-native video (like an embedded

YouTube video), native video (a video posted directly to Facebook), slide decks, photo albums, and more. Facebook is constantly adding new ways of creating status updates.

- **Tabs**: Somewhat misnamed, Tabs are just navigational links that allow you to add easy access to other parts of your Facebook page. *Tabs* live in two places on your Facebook Page; on the left side of your timeline and in the navigation bar under your cover photo. Tabs can also be used to host a variety of Facebook apps, which help a business extend their capabilities directly on their Facebook Page. These can include Facebook contests, connections other social media accounts, hosting a storefront, or much more. To see what is available and choose apps to add to your page's tabs, visit the Facebook App Center. You can also control which Tabs are shown in what order, essentially organizing your Facebook micro-site how you'd like.

   How you use your tab space is a question that needs to be answered by your social strategy. Different goals, such as driving webpage traffic or collecting leads, will inform your choices.

- **Insights**: These are visible only to the page admins and are the core analytics for your page. This tab allows marketers to see the key performance indicators (KPIs) associated with their activity on their Facebook Page. These analytics help you identify your audience, see which posts get the most engagement, and track the volume of your fan building activity.

I've included a handy size guide under Resources at *A SocialMedia.Pro* for you to use in setting up your Profile and Cover photos. http://bit.ly/1XF6Itp

Apps

Facebook apps are little add-ons that you can use to flesh out your page. With them you can do things like add your Instagram pictures, add chat functions, or add surveys or polls. Like all apps, some are free and some are paid. Here are a few of my favorites (I don't do games, so no Candy Crush Saga on this list):

1. **Aviary**: The basic image editing tools at Aviary.com aren't exactly a full verion of Photoshop, but they are good enough for most purposes. This app allows you to crop, resize, change brightness or contrast or saturation, draw upon, type a caption, fix redeye, and apply effects to any image in your albums or on your timeline.
2. **Norton Safe Web**: Especially useful if you're allowing posts by others. Safe Web checks your Facebook wall for things like malicious links. Run the scan and it will check all your

links and warn you if there's a reason for concern.

3. **iFrapp**: A DIY app builder, iFrapp can build contests, contact forms, showrooms, video players, and more using simple online tools. It'll cost you a minimum of $15 a month to have one app.

4. **Facebook Video Calling**: Facebook's new Video Calling feature uses Skype technology to get you face-to-face with friends fast. To start chatting, find any online friend in your chat list and click the camera logo next to the person's name. Facebook will make you download and install a little plug-in

5. **ShortStack**: Another popular app builder, it lets you create social media contests and marketing campaigns.

6. **Buffer**: Yep. Buffer's got an app for post planning as well.

7. **Fan-Of-The-Week**: Each week a fan is picked from among those who interacted with your page by liking, posting or commenting. The selection happens automatically. It's a great way to recognize and encourage engagement on your page.

8. **Surveymonkey**: Use SurveyMonkey surveys and their Facebook Collector or Web Link Collector to create and deliver surveys to friends, fans and customers.

Page Button

Facebook recently added a function that allows you to create a call-to-action button at the bottom right of your cover photo. You can, for example add a, *"Shop Now,"* button with a link to your website, or a, *"Contact Us,"* with a link to your contact page. These are extremely useful and should not be ignored.

Here's Jay Baer's header. Notice the *Follow* button. Other options include Call Now, Contact Us, Send Email Send Message, Book Now, Shop Now, Sign Up, Play Game, Use App, and Watch Video.

Reviews & Testimonials

Another great resource for syndicating content are reviews and testimonials. Whether you realize it or not, reviews are critical to your livelihood. Your website should absolutely have a place for customers to leave reviews, but far more valuable are getting reviews on Google + and Facebook as you can see by the graphic below.

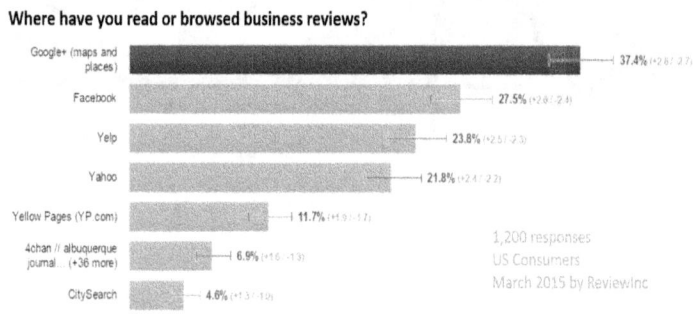

Where have you read or browsed business reviews?

Google+ (maps and places)	37.4% (+28/-27)
Facebook	27.5% (+28/-24)
Yelp	23.8% (+25/-23)
Yahoo	21.8% (+24/-22)
Yellow Pages (YP.com)	11.7% (+19/-17)
4chan // albuquerque journal (+36 more)	6.9% (+16/-13)
CitySearch	4.6% (+13/-10)

1,200 responses
US Consumers
March 2015 by ReviewInc

Because these reviews are seen as uncensored, they carry more weight with the reader. Google also uses your reviews on their site in determining your worthiness for presenting your site link in your search return pages (SERPs).

It is important that you encourage your customers during the close to write a review for you. There is never a better time to have them write a review during that honeymoon right after closing the sale.

Note: I know we're focused on Facebook, but a quick word about Google+ reviews. DON'T sign up the customer for a new Google account just to get a review; always use an existing Google account. If they have an @gmail.com email, they have a Google account. If they have an Android phone they have an @gmail.com account. Your reviews will get tossed if there are a bunch of new Google users who have only ever posted a single review for you. You can't trick the system. One of our clients tried this method (against our advice), and after about 2-months they got 87 reviews deleted.

Google also tracks the IP address that the review comes from. So setting up a kiosk, or having all the reviews written in your office on your tablet, is also going to be an exercise in futility. Google will simply flag all the reviews as coming from the same IP address and throw them away. Google's main policy is that if there is any doubt as to the veracity of the review, they'll discard it. No second chances. No appeals.

Facebook is far more forgiving about reviews and sources than Google. Most users of mobile devices are using the Facebook app anyway, so having them add a short review right there in your dealership, right in front of you on their smartphone is simple and quick.

Responding

One of the biggest reasons marketers give for ignoring comments and reviews online is a fear of having to respond. They are reluctant to get involved with a customer in a public forum; they see this as setting a dangerous precedent. They aren't sure what to say. They don't want to say the wrong thing.

Here's the blunt truth; saying nothing is absolutely the wrong thing. Every time and under every circumstance. Failure to comment or reply is almost always seen as an admission of guilt. Brands start out guilty on the Internet, anyway. It's important that you take the time to respond to public criticism publicly and reasonably. That means no personal attacks, no blaming the victim (even if they aren't really the victim), and no getting angry. Even if their post is untrue, it's important to remain calm and be SEEN to be the reasonable one.

This is how you reverse the *companies are always wrong*, perception. Once you become the reasonable one, other Facebook users will turn on the original poster. Let them get angry for you. Let them say the things that you desperately want to, but can't. Well shouldn't, anyway.

Here are a few tips on how to respond:

- Respond quickly and accurately.
- Show gratitude and respect. Never, ever respond in a negative or offensive way.
- Include facts and data, not opinions. If it's possible to link to factual data, do so but don't expose personal information about the commenter.
- Respond in a tone of voice that reflects the company's values and culture.
- Be transparent. Let the commenter know how you're connected with the company. Never pretend to be a customer, if you aren't. In fact, never pretend to be anything or anyone you are not.

It's also important that you have a response policy in place. The easiest thing to do is to assign one person to monitor comments and reviews and give that person the authority and responsibility of replying.

A better, but more involved, solution is to give everyone the authority and the necessary training to speak to reviews and comments. I believe this is the best solution, though obviously training becomes an integral aspect of how they respond and when.

You've probably heard the maxim, "Don't feed the trolls." Trolls are online commenters who do so broadly, without specifics and often in the most offensive ways possible. These are the guys who post things like, "I hate these people," or "Such-and-Such company sucks." You'd rarely if ever use the word, *articulate*, to refer to a post from a troll.

I'm of the opinion that there are times you should feed the trolls, or more specifically their detractors... people I call the *troll hunters*. Troll hunters are just waiting to take a bite out of the first troll that comes along. While the times to break out the troll bait are few, where a troll actually has something to say, you can respond as shown below.

There are four things you can do with any comment or review; ignore, acknowledge, respond, or ban/report. You should also definitely make use of the settings on your Facebook page to do two things; first set *Visitor Postings* to, *Review posts by other people before they are published to the page.* Second set the Profanity Filter to *Strong.* This will automatically kill many trollish comments, since these often include profanity such as "You f@°ing suck."

Let's look at the most common scenarios in turn:

- Positive & False: Thank them for their comments, but don't correct the misinformation unless it is directly tied to your presence, such as hours or location.
- Positive + True: Thank them for their comments.
- Negative + Troll: "You suck," doesn't exactly give you a lot of room for engagement. Trollish comments like this should be deleted and the troll banned. For reviews, if there is any use of profanity or any other violation of Facebook rules you can report it. Otherwise, since you can't delete Reviews, ignore those kind of reviews. No good with come from engaging on this.
- Negative + Not a Troll + Erroneous/Untrue: Correct the misinformation as politely and directly as possible.
- Negative + Not a Troll + True: This is where a sincere, "I'm

sorry," carries a lot of weight. Add a, *"Please contact me directly so I can try to resolve the issue and re-earn your trust."* Simple and direct.

Create Benchmarks for Your Brand

The volume of negative feedback you receive is influenced by a number of factors including how much reach you get, the size and quality of your audience, and the specific industry segment you represent. All these factors are unique for your company. I suggest you determine your acceptable feedback levels and establish benchmarks based on the average volume of negative feedback you receive by post.

You need to set goals for decreasing your negative feedback to help maximize your post reach. You should also look at how your organic posts measure up against your paid posts. One of my clients gets more negative feedback on paid posts than organic posts. So we know that monitoring the paid posts is critical so that we can respond accordingly.

This information becomes especially interesting when you're serving up the same post on both organic and paid; for example, on a boosted post. Is there something about your ad targeting strategy that's causing this? How do your organic and paid posts compare over time? This type of negative feedback measurement will become especially important as social marketers of all stripes decide to put more money towards Facebook ad spend.

Facebook Messenger

Recently Facebook introduced several new features for Facebook Messenger, which can be used to make contacting your brand easier. These include Usernames, Links and Messenger Codes. The best thing about these new features, in my opinion, is that phone numbers aren't necessary, and you don't have to be friends on Facebook.

These new features are going to allow your customers and prospects to start conversations immediately. Here's how they work:

Messenger Codes are one of the easiest ways to find people and be found in Messenger. It doesn't matter if you are standing next to them, or on the other side of the world looking at your computer screen. No matter where you are all you have to do is share the scanable code with your audience and they can connect to you in a couple of clicks.

No more back and forth with texts trying to make sure you have the right number saved and awkwardly asking people how to spell their names. Your settings tab in Messenger has your own Messenger Code displayed prominently to scan or share.

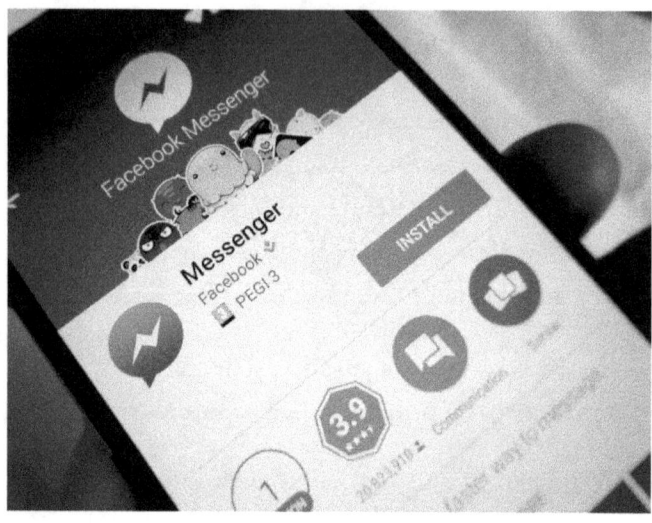

Sharing can be done online, in emails, or in print. For example, try adding your Messenger code to the back of your business cards, or to your flyers and other ads. Even on in-store posters. How about adding them next to your buyer's guides, or on rack cards and other marketing materials? Certainly, add them to your web pages.

Messenger Links and Usernames are also personalized links that you can share anywhere online - from your email signature to your website. You can send your Messenger Link directly to your contacts or friends. Tap or click any Messenger Link to open Messenger directly to a thread with that person or business. We are all unique human beings, but sometimes we share the same name! This can make it hard to know you are contacting the right person when searching for them in Messenger. Now, it's simple to find someone by his or her very own unique username. You can find and share your username from your Settings tab. It will look something like this — m.me/username.

Of course using messenger provides you with one more contact pipeline for your customers. Phone, text, messages, Facebook comments; these are all just open conduits to start the conversation. The more you have, the easier it becomes for your customers and prospects to connect with.

Automating Messenger

Facebook has recently added what they call, "Instant Replies." These are canned responses you can use to respond to Messenger automatically when you aren't available. For example, during the hours you are closed. A little like a way to use artificial intelligence to help ensure you are replying in a timely manner.

You create these instant replies through the Response Assistant. To get there go to Setting and select Messenger. Scroll to the bottom of the page and you'll see the Response Assistant. You can set up responses for multiple different possible scenarios. On the next page you'll see an example of I set up for one client.

Response Assistant

Response Time

Currently set to "Typically takes more than a day to reply"

Change

> You need to respond to at least 75% of the messages within a day or less to show response time on your page.
> Currently set to "Typically takes more than a day to reply" with 68% response rate.

Set status to 'Away' outside business hours

This will let customers know when you're unable to respond promptly.

Yes

Enable Away Messages

Create a message that's automatically sent to people when your status is set to 'Away' or it's outside your business hours.

Yes

Change

> "Sorry, Clifford we're closed right now, but I'll have someone get back to yu as soon as we open. You can also call the store at (269) 441-6100 or check our website http://www.expressauto.com/."

Send Instant Replies to anyone who messages your Page

Instant Replies are a good way to let people know that you'll respond soon.

Yes

Change

> "Thanks, Clifford . Your essage is being relayed to one of our program advisors. They will get back to you shortly. What's a good number to call you back?"

As long as you have entered your business hours into your business page, you'll be able to use these auto responders.

You can even personalize the responses, so they sound less like a canned response and more like a person. You can choose to embed the person's first name, last name, your website URL, your phone number, or your address. Where we've used the

Person's first name

Person's last name

Your website URL

Your phone number

Your address

first name, your phone, and you website URL, s sample auto-responder
would look like this:

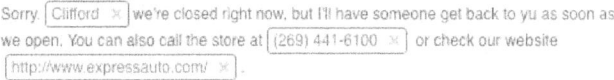

The message would look like this:

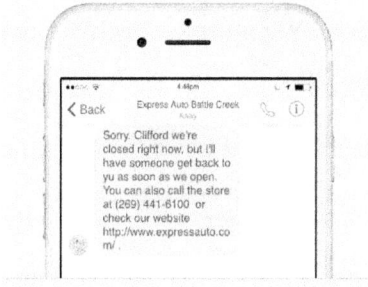

Going Prospecting

You get started on social prospecting by establishing your social presence. You do this by providing your Facebook fans with more than just an endless stream of sales pitches. It's important that you become part of their community.

At the same time you need to recognize that social media can be a huge time suck, unless you put processes in place to automate and control your Facebook presence.

Here are a few general rules I use to make sure that I'm not overspending resources on managing Facebook.

- Use the 5/1 rule. For every selling post you put out through your profile or page, you should be posting four posts that have nothing to do with your product. These can be targeted to ensure maximum shares. All you have to do is look at your customer profile to identify their interests. If you are running Google PPC (pay per click) through Google Adwords, you can use Google to help you identify the kinds of things that your prospects are searching for. For example, if they are interested in cooking or restaurants, post about those things. Sports? Sure. Even if these things aren't related directly to what you're selling, they will bring in interested fans.

- Use the One-Two-Three method to keep your time spent on Facebook to a minimum, but get maximum effect. That is:
  - One. At least one fresh post each day. This can be curated or create content. A link, a video, a picture, etc. Something that wasn't there on your page or profile the day before.
  - Two. At least two comments or shares on posts by other people. This helps you build community. Ideally find things that your customers are already interested in and talking about. Get involved in the conversation.
  - Three. Try to "Like" at least three posts by other people.

If all that takes you more than 10-minutes a day, you're doing it wrong. There are also free sites out there to help you manage your system. One of my favorites is a web-app called Buffer (http://bufferapp.com). Using Buffer and the Buffer Chrome Browser Add-on, I can queue things to be posted at a later time to any Facebook page or Twitter account I manage. So, I can find a bunch of interesting things and schedule curated posts out for the whole week.

I use Buffer to schedule curated posts like photos, links, and videos twice a day; at 9AM and at 6PM. Then I fill in throughout the week with some created content.

I use another free online app called Pocket to help me find interesting stuff to share. I put anything interesting in my Pocket queue to review later. Pocket also gives me recommendations based on links I've already saved.

When I have time, I pull up Pocket (https://getpocket.com/a/queue/) and review the links or videos, then Buffer them for posting. Like Buffer, Pocket also has a Chrome add-on that makes saving things as easy as a single click.

The final point of my trident of tools is something called Zapier (https://zapier.com/). Zapier allows you to create ZAPs. If/Then links between web applications. So you can create a Zap that takes anything you post on your blog and shares it to your Facebook page automatically. Or a Zap that takes new content from your YouTube channel and pushes it to Twitter. The possibilities are endless and best of all, automatic. It takes a few minutes to create and test the zaps, but once done you are on autopilot with your posting.

Facebook itself also gives you some management tools for your posts. The save for later function lets you save videos or photos for later. Pull them up again, and then Buffer them for distribution. So you can schedule posts for later right in Facebook.

The Dangers of Over-Automation

We touched on using auto-replies as a way of automating Facebook Messenger when you're not around. This is a great way to automate what you're doing in Facebook. So are the suggestions above, but you must be careful about overusing automation techniques on social media.

One of the goals of conversation marketing is to present yourself as human. Too much automation will create a stream that has no human voice. This de-humanizing works directly against the whole idea of conversation marketing. Make sure that the posts that are automated are personal enough that your audience does not see you as a spam account. Finding the middle ground between staying in the conversation and automated posts is the key to success.

Remember – once you have set up social media automation, you can't just forget about it. To have a successful account, you need to monitor your progress. You have to keep connected and engaged with your audience from the beginning to the end. From your first post to your last.

Understanding which parts of social media to automate can be a challenge. Remember the Rule of 5? Out of every five posts you do, up to three can be content from someone else, but at least one should be content from you that is relevant, but not a sales pitch. The last one of the five can be sales oriented. At least two of those posts should be something that makes you seem more human and more approachable. Keep it funny, entertaining or educational.

One way of working the social media automation system (and keeping a 'human' voice) is automating posts that are not that important.

Examples of this would be, quotes or memes. These can be automated at times of the day where you're away. These kinds of posts will make sense at any time and continue to humanize your online presence since they tend to be humorous.

The aim of automated posts is to maintain a presence. Posts like quotes and memes aren't going to be seen as spam so long as you mix them up with more topical posts.

There are definitely times when you shouldn't use automated posts; such as in dealing with customer relations. The way you respond to customers online can mean the difference between keeping and losing a customer. People like to be talked to by other humans not by an automated robot.

Facebook made much out of their recent launch of BOTs, artificial intelligence programs that can respond to simple customer requests. I'd approach incorporating BOTs and auto-responders into your social presence with caution.

Facebook the Advertising Platform

Effective online advertising can be measured in two ways; conversions and overall ROI. When it comes to effective online advertising, there is no more powerful resource than Facebook.

When you think about it, Facebook is the most popular and most visited social media site in the world. Advertise on Facebook and you are advertising to a potential audience of more than a billion people.

If you have never created a Facebook campaign before then you may have some questions before you start. *Will Facebook ads work for my business?*

This is the first thing that many people want to know about Facebook ads. No matter what industry you are in, Facebook ads when properly configured and targeted will work. This is because Facebook has people from all over the world and from all walks of life on its website. More importantly, it allows you to target people geographically, and demographically so that you are talking to the people most receptive to your message.

There is a common misconception that only certain types of businesses can sell or prospect on Facebook. Small and large businesses alike have convinced themselves it'll never work. Some have even tried it without getting the results they expected. I've spent millions on behalf of clients and I can tell you this: Facebook advertising, when properly targeted is the most effective online advertising available at this time.

Millions of CEOs, housewives, blue and white-collar workers, and consumers in general are all on Facebook. If you are worried about reaching the right people with, forget about it. Your customers and prospects are right there, on Facebook, every day. Even if you assume your typical customer isn't a Facebook user, you may be surprised to find they are on the site just waiting for you to take their pain away. *What should my goal be for Facebook ads?*

There is really only one goal you should have for any online advertising campaign; ***Conversions***. You're not going to sell cars online, I won't say it's not possible (EBay Motors), but that's probably not your business model. Converting Facebook ads to leads is the main goal that most of us should be targeting. Converting them in a traceable way, so you can follow the sales cycle all the way through to the delivery, is the holy grail.

Facebook advertising is a great platform because it puts you in touch with all types of potential customers and because it is really easy to use. Just because Facebook ads are relatively easy and affordable, you shouldn't just jump into a new campaign without proper pre-planning. If you want Facebook ads to work in the way they are supposed to, then you need to start the process with a this clear goal in mind. You need to have a precise understanding of what it is that you want to accomplish with your ads.

- Do you want new customers? How many?
- Do you want more visits to your website?
- Are you looking to get people to register for an event?

The more specific you are with your goals, the more you can tailor your ads to help you reach your goals, and the more you can track your progress to make necessary changes to your ads.

If you want to find success with your Facebook ads, then you need to know your KPIs (*Key Performance Indicators*). Now I've just stated that conversions is the only goal really worth anything, but traceable conversions lead you to being able to make other conclusions about your Facebook ads and change your approach as needed.

You don't want to get caught up trying to drive down your cost per click to 10 cents if that means you are going to make fewer sales, or less profit per sale. Also, you want to make sure your investment is fully optimized for conversions (leads or sales) to maximize your ROI. You have to avoid being trapped at the wrong end the "Hockey Stick Distribution," but more about that in a minute.

Keep proper metrics on your Facebook marketing and you can often turn $1 into $20 once you have a campaign dialed in. The key is being able to track which specific leads came from Facebook into your CRM, and follow them through to the delivery. That's going to give you a cost per lead and cost per sale using simple division.

Overall your cost per sale should not exceed $200. If you are seeing a cost per sale below $200 you're not investing enough to see the highest conversion rate possible. Above that, and you've gone too far.

Another indicator you need to track is time to sale. In other words, the length of time from the date the lead came into the system, to the date of the actual delivery. Some leads have a much longer selling cycle than other. By tracking this, you help confirm whether a campaign is call-to-action or branding. Both are valid campaigns, but to get the best results you'll want to create a proper mix with fewer branding ads and more call-to-action ads for better and faster conversion.

One last metric that is important to follow is closing percentage. This is an indicator of how well your salespeople are doing at closing the lead once it's in the system. A low closing rate, typically below 6%, is the sign of either poor lead quality (you can't qualify them for some reason and see a high percentage of turn-downs), or poor salesmanship. For the first, you need to look at your financing set up. The second involves professional development training. So we're going to track the following:

- Conversions (Leads/Viewers = Conversions).
- Cost per Lead (Spend/Total Leads = CPL)
- Cost per Sale (Spend/Delivered = CPS)
- Sale Cycle (Date In CRM - Date Delivered= SC = Sell Cycle)
- Closing % (Delivered/Total Leads = CL)

Optimizing

All Facebook ads work on a pay-per-click basis, so to optimize your advertising investment you don't just want *more* clicks, you want the *right* clicks. One way to make sure you're getting the right clicks is to watch your bounce rate in your website analytics. If you start running an ad and your bounce rate increases by more than 5%, you can bet that ad is getting a lot of clicks from the wrong people; people who aren't interested in your message. Remember, it's better to talk with 100 people who care about your message than 100,000 people who don't

One of the biggest mistakes that you can make when creating Facebook ads is to target too large a group of potential customers. Yes, Facebook gives you access to millions and millions of potential customers, but you want to make sure that you take advantage of PIT (*Precise Interest Targeting*) to really focus in on who will see your ads. Targeting the largest group possible is a mistake.

When targeting an audience you can focus on defining characteristics of your ideal customers, including their likes and interests, the pages they follow, the apps they use, and more. You will need to do some research yourself and look for individual publications and blogs your ideal customer will likely follow and you use this insight to focus in on what pages your customers likely follow.

Here is one of the most effective ways to ensure your ads are getting to the right people. Simply target people who already like a competitor's page and coattail on the work they've done. That assumes of course, they've done any work.

Another way is to focus on large employers in your area where you know you have a number of customers already.

Of course the easiest way is to use a Facebook custom audience and also target a lookalike audience. Something we'll cover in detail shortly.

Facebook has robust targeting abilities—you can target people based on a variety of information shared in their profile, and the activities they perform on the platform— from interests and behavior, down to zip

code and more. You can also create *Custom Audiences*, which allow you
to target users a couple of different ways:

1. By Customer List: Match emails, or phone numbers from
   your CRM to people on Facebook
2. By Website Traffic: Create a list of people who visit your
   website or specific web pages.

If you have a marketing automation platform or CRM that integrates
with Facebook it's possible to tightly intertwine your paid Facebook ads
directly with your other ongoing digital marketing campaigns. For
example, it could help you better target "known" customers based on
information from your marketing automation platform. Or, it could
help you engage unknown audiences by using personalization data from
across channels to send targeted Facebook ads to users.

Creating Facebook Ad Campaigns

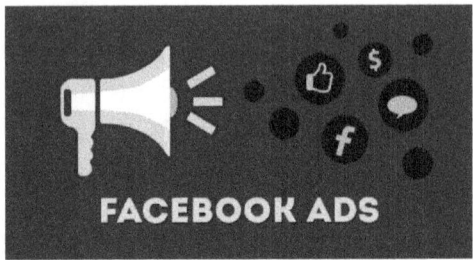

As you can see lead generation doesn't have to stop with what we've outlined in the prospecting section. Even on a relatively modest budget, adding Facebook advertising to your mix is a no-brainer. Your ads should support your other efforts, reaching out to drive traffic to your website, as well as generate leads directly. There are three kinds of ads I recommend using as part of your online mix. We'll be going over each of these individually in more detail, but here's an overview:

- **Boosted Posts.** The optimum type of boosted post is video. Walk-around videos and explainer videos (your value proposition presented as an explainer video is a great option). As we've discussed, each of these videos should include captions, and a button link at the end, such as *Shop Now*, or *Sign Up*. Depending on the time of day and Facebook's opinion of your post's relevance you might only reach 10% of your audience organically. Boosted posts allow you to reach a larger audience.

- **Local Awareness Ads.** What makes these ads great is that you can easily include a Click-to-Call button on the ad. Since most people will see these ads on a mobile device, you'll drive phone calls more than web-hits As long as your people are properly trained on phone skills, you can see a huge boost in leads from these incoming calls.

- **Lead Ads.** My new favorites since I discovered how to link Lead Ads with Zapier Zaps to deliver leads directly as they come in. Lead ads incorporate a form, which Facebook makes easy to complete on mobile devices. These forms save the lead information to the Forms Library under your Publishing Tools on your page. By automating with Zapier, you can have them delivered right to your manager or sales team for real-time follow-up.

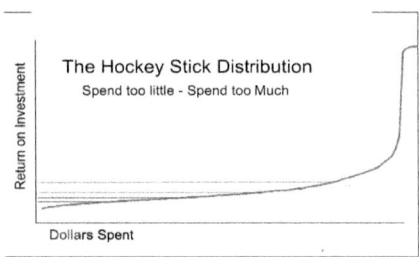

Obviously, the more you invest in running the ads, the more leads you'll see… to a point. Beware of what I call the hockey-stick distribution. Too small a budget will produce disappointing results. There's a point where results will begin to shoot up markedly, but there's also a point of diminishing returns where more budget doesn't produce much better results.

As you can see in the chart above, when you spend too little you get caught too far on the left side of the distribution. As you move to the right, you see a sharp return on investment. Then eventual lower returns as you follow the curve past the peak ROI.

You have to be aware of other KPIs (*key performance indicators*), such as cost per lead, cost per sale, and sell cycle (how long it takes for a lead to generate a sale). Paying attention to these indicators will allow you to ensure the best ROI on your advertising.

Experiment and you'll find the best spot on the hockey stick for your budget.

Creating Audiences

Step one in building your Facebook ads isn't creating the ads. Before you start building ads, you need to build audiences. Audiences are just what they sound like. They are the targets of your advertising.

Facebook gives you a lot of targeting options right out of the box. You can target by age, gender, location, interests and more. You can also use partner data (like Datalogix) and target by life events/behaviors, net worth/income, political affiliation and household composition. One of the best ways to start is by geographically targeting your audience. For your dealership, there's an excellent chance that the preponderance of your customers come from a geographic zone of 22-25 miles. Facebook allows you to set a geographic targeting radius.

Once you've targeted geographically, you can also target demographically. Start with age range, and then add other factors such as interests or income. Again, before you approach any advertising, online or offline, you need to have a clear customer profile. You need to know how far away they are coming from, what age they are, etc. If you don't have that, you don't have a place to start from.

You can also import your own data, such as website visitors, current customers, high value customers, loyalty club members and valuable leads. This last category is where *Facebook Custom Audiences* come into the picture. Facebook Custom Audiences are lists of people who are already part of your audience. These are your current customers, past purchasers, high value customers, loyalty program members, warm leads, etc.

There is also *Website Custom Audiences.* These are lists of people who have visited your website (or certain pages on it), and taken certain actions. If you have emails, and phone numbers, Facebook finds those people so you can use Custom Audiences as a targeting option to reach them with specific ads.

For example, you can present a special offer only to people who have looked at your inventory online, or create a downloadable coupon for only current customers. You can even target those past customers you haven't heard from for a while, with a special buy again offer.

Sure, you can target these people already using email or even by phone, but people check their Facebook newsfeed up to 15 times per day. Facebook becomes one more arrow in your quiver; one more way to connect with your customers and potential customers.

Facebook's most powerful targeting option is Custom Audiences Facebook ad targeting is very powerful. They have so much data available to help advertisers narrow down their audience.

To create custom audiences from a Data File, you need to get that data. Get the data from your customers, whether it is emails or user IDs. You can upload the data in CSV (comma separated values -- a common spreadsheet format), so make sure you have only one type of data per file using emails or phone numbers. You can upload this to Facebook, but be sure to read through the Facebook Custom Audiences terms. Make sure you've gotten all the data legally and with the consent of the user. You can get penalized if you are scraping data.

In order to use a website custom audience, you will need to have a custom audience pixel, which is a snippet of code you put into your website source code.

When you have the pixel installed on your website, it triggers every time someone does any of the actions you specify. If you want more information on how to customize it, go to this Custom Audiences overview page (http://tinyurl.com/za2uvw2).

A couple things worth mentioning:

1. Custom Audiences can take up to 36 hours to fully process.
2. Facebook doesn't deliver ads to audiences of less than 20 people.

When you look at the list of custom audiences, it will tell you the name and the estimated audience size, but audience size is not always accurate on Facebook.

Lookalike Audiences

Another powerful aspect of creating a custom audience is the ability to build a lookalike audience.

A lookalike audience is exactly what it sounds like, a target group who demographically and geographically resemble a custom audience you've already created. One of the best ways to use a lookalike audience is to simply upload your customer list and create a lookalike audience to target people who are similar to people who have already bought from you. Facebook recently expanded lookalike audiences to include people who like your Facebook page, website visitors and mobile app users.

- To find more people who look like your website visitors —
  Now you can use data from your Facebook pixels (Facebook
  Conversion Pixel or the Custom Audiences for Websites

pixel) to reach people who are most similar to people who previously made purchases on your website. E-commerce company Shopify saw a 2X decrease in cost per lead when using lookalikes of their website visitors.

• Conversation marketing is about engaging customers and prospects. Now you can target lookalike audiences to reach people like the fans already connected to your Facebook Page(s)

So how do we harness the power of lookalikes for your business? That requires us to take a trip to the Power Editor under Facebook's Manage Ads menu. Here's a step-by-step guide —

• First, click the Ad Tools drop-down at the top right of Power Editor and select "Audiences."

• Next, click the Create Audience drop-down at the top left and select "Lookalike Audience."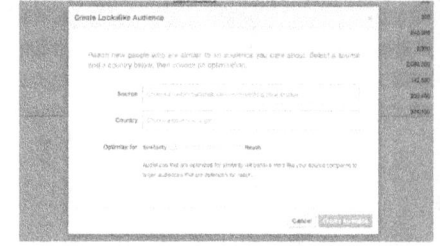

• That will give you a dialog box that looks like the image on the next page.

1.   Within the "Source" text box, you can select a page that you're the Admin for or a Custom Audience (including a Website Custom Audience) or a or Conversion Pixel (more about conversion pixels in a moment).

2.   Finally, use the slider to determine whether you want to optimize for Similarity or Reach. In the past, Facebook only gave you the option of one or the other. Now you can pick your audience size.

Once that Lookalike Audience is ready, you can target it in your ads. This is done within the Custom Audiences text field of the "Audience" step of ad creation.

Conversion Pixels

I mentioned using conversion pixels above and I want to go a little more in depth into exactly how they are useful. Conversion pixels are really a remarketing tool, allowing you to target people who have been to your website on Facebook as part of a custom audience.

Many users of Website Custom Audiences get confused. You might think they need to install a different pixel to each page, depending on the audience. Understand that you have only one pixel per ad account, and that same pixel needs to be on all pages of your website (or websites).

Creating the rules for a specific Website Custom Audience will determine which website visitors you target with which ads.

Creating the pixel is easy and quick:

- Within Ads Manager, select "Audiences" within the Tools drop-down at the top.
- If you've ever created Custom Audiences before, you'll see the "Create Audience" drop-down. Select "Custom Audience."
- Click the "Create a Custom Audience" button.
- If you've never created a Custom Audience of any kind before, you'll get a popover. Select "Website Traffic."
    - o If you've never attempted to create a Website Custom Audience before, you'll first be asked to accept Facebook's Terms for Custom Audiences.
- If you haven't added the pixel to your site yet and are instead taken to the Create Pixel process, click the gear icon at the bottom and select *View Pixel Code*.
- You'll then be given your advertising account's unique Website Custom Audience pixel. Paste this between the *<head></head>* tags of the page you want to track.
- Now that the pixel is properly installed on every page of you want to track, you can use it to create some Website Custom Audiences. Now let's go back to the Ads Manager where you had

previously copied the pixel code.

- Click the button to "Create Audience."

Start by generating an audience of people who visited a specific landing page, your vehicle details pages (VDPs) or a group of pages for targeting.

- Simply enter the URL(s) you want to include. Anyone who visited those URLs will be added to your audience.

- You'll see options for *URL contains* and *URL equals*. Here's the difference. When *URL contains* is selected, you can enter a partial URL and capture visitors to multiple related pages; e.g. if my URL structure was web.com/vehicle/2008_ford-explorer. I could build an audience of all people who visited any page with web.com/vehicles/.

- Let's say you want to track a specific page such as the thank you page that's presented after they download a coupon. You'd use URL equals and enter the exact URL of that page. For example, you could use that data to target everyone who has downloaded a coupon and remind them of the expiration.

Don't slice the pie too thin. Facebook won't run ads to an audience of less than 20, and remember what I said earlier about audience size not being accurate in the projected numbers Facebook shows when you set your audience.

Building Ads

Now that you have your audience set up and saved, you can start building ads. I'm going to walk you through each of the ad types step-by-step so you have a clear understanding of how to set up each and the advantages that each offers.

It's important to use a mix of at least two of these ad types, since each one has a slightly different appeal, even if you are aiming them at the same audience. While consistency of visual branding is important, I do recommend you change up the general look of each ad. You see the problem with billboards. After a week or two, response rates from billboards will begin to drop markedly because once you've seen and processed the imagery, your brain pushes it out of the way.

So different visuals become important to attracting different and changing up the message is equally important. Ads should run for no more than a week or two at the most, then get changed up.

Creating an ad is as simple as clicking on the arrow icon in the top right corner of your Facebook screen and choosing *create ad*.

Advertising Design 101

Whether you're a skillful designer, or just a beginner, there are a few things to make sure you include in your ad layout. This is basic advertising design, whether you're building a banner ad, a flyer or any of these different types of Facebook ads.

- Colors and general design elements consistent with your brand should definitely include at least a good-sized logo.
- Value proposition or offer. Again, a no brainer. "What's in it for me?" What do I get? Why should I be interested? The best value propositions are eight words or less.
- Call-to-action. People are naturally drawn to a button. It's a conditioned response to want to click on it. Sign Up Now! Or Get Your Free Download!

	Recommended Image Size
Clicks to Website	1,200 x 628 pixels
Website Conversions	1,200 x 628 pixels
Page Post Engagement	1,200 x 900 pixels
Page Likes	1,200 x 444 pixels
App Installs	1,200 x 628 pixels
App Engagement	1,200 x 628 pixels
Local Awareness	1,200 x 628 pixels
Event Responses	1,200 x 444 pixels
Offer Claims	1,200 x 628 pixels
Video Views	1,200 x 675 pixels

It's also important to realize that your ads will be seen on a number of different platforms and at a number of different screen sizes. You should take care to make certain that the images you use are properly sized so that they will look good. Refer to the handy guide above to for the optimum image size for each ad type.

As you can see, if you keep your images at least 1200 pixels wide by 900 pixels tall, you'll be good in most cases. Just realize that on smaller screens some top and bottom cropping might occur. It's always easier to take something bigger and make it smaller, but the reverse is not true. Making a smaller image larger will cause it to break up, what's called artifacting or pixilation. This looks very unprofessional.

Boosted Posts

These are the easiest kind of ad to create. There is a Boost Post button on every post you put on your page. Obviously not every post deserves to be boosted, but remember that one out of five posts that can be a sale pitch? You can turn these easily into ads with one click.

Facebook gives you a few options with boosted posts. Here's an overview of choices I recommend:

- Apply your audience to the ad,
- Boost posts for no more than 7-days to prevent visual immunity from setting in.
- Pay attention to how your budget affects the audience size. Remember the hockey-stick distribution. Try different amounts to see the results and settle on the one with the best ROI.

That's about it for boosted posts. The lack of options beyond audience targeting and budget is what makes them so simple to do. Be careful you don't fall into the trap of **only** using boosted posts, though.

Our other two major ad types might take a little longer to set up, but you'll see different results with each.

One more thing about boosted posts. There are two special types of posts that you can also boost. These are events and offers.

Let's say you have a special tent sale coming up, you'd make this an event post and boost it exactly the same way you'd boost any other post.

If you want to offer a special coupon or discount, you can make this an offer post with a link to download the coupon off your website. This is a great way to track the response rate since you can require them to bring the coupon in to get the discount. Count the coupons and compare it to the ad's viewer stats and you have your numbers.

Local Awareness Ads

These ads are meant to help build your brand in your local service area, but have the advantage of incorporating a call-now button for call-to-action marketing. Since as much as 90% of your ad activity will take place on the Facebook mobile app, the call-now button can drive a lot of incoming phone calls. I highly suggest using a separate phone line that you only use for these ads so you can accurately cross-reference incoming calls to what Facebook registers as click-to-call clicks.

Being able to cross reference the incoming numbers from the phone bill to leads in your CRM allows you to get a solid feel for more than just how well the ads are performing, it allows you to track how well your staff is performing at getting the a real leads from the call. That means getting a name and phone number from every incoming sales call. If they aren't doing this, the ad performance is irrelevant.

Local awareness ads are slightly more complicated to set up, especially since I recommend you run them on a schedule and not continuously.

Remember what I said about visual immunity? I believe strongly that running the same ad continuously is going to kill the effectiveness of the ad over time.

The easiest way to get started is to look in your left sidebar. You'll likely see a Promote Local Business button floating there. You could click that amd be off and running, but it offers you fewer options than you need.

- Instead, go to the Ad Manager and select *Create New Campaign*. From the next page choose, *Reach People Near Your Business* to create a new local awareness campaign with more options.
- If you manage multiple pages, Facebook will then give you the option to choose which business you want to promote. Then choose set *Audience and Budget.*
- From the next page you'll set the radius for your business. Again, I'd recommend 20-25 miles for most dealers. You'll also target age and gender.
- The real key difference between setting up here and using the more convenient Promote Local Business button is the next section. Budget and schedule. Change Daily Budget to Lifetime Budget and you'll see the Schedule section appear.
- Set your ad to run between the dates you want it to appear. Again, I recommend you run the ad for no more than 14-days.

I can't stress enough that these are great ads that can be rendered utterly irrelevant if your phone system isn't properly configured and if your employees aren't properly trained to get the lead FIRST on an incoming call.

Determine Which Posts to Boost

It is especially important for boosted posts that you take the time to determine which posts are worthy of investing your advertising dollars in. After all, putting money down on the wrong horse will just influence you to believe all horse racing is bad. Before you start allocating ad dollars, you need to determine which content is worth promoting.

The more insights you glean ahead of time, the greater the likelihood of success when you execute.

1. Analyze your content over an historical period (three, six, or even nine months) and give new life to well performing old content. Such as posts with high engagement and click counts. These top-performing posts have the potential to be more successful when boosted.

2. As counterintuitive as it might sound, give lower-performing content one last chance by identifying posts that drove little or no engagement, but took a lot of effort or resources to put together. Use Facebook ads to reframe that content and give it new life. For example, change the audience target, or pair the content with a new offer. Then put that content out to pasture for good if it still doesn't perform.

3. Analyze your competitor's' Facebook content to determine which content performs well with your target audience. Look to

their comments and shares to determine this easily. Then copy the gist of that content, not the content itself. Identifying top performers and understanding what content your competitors use to successfully drive engagement and clicks gives you more options when putting together your promoted-content strategy.

4. Take a look at other platforms like YouTube or Twitter. Determining what works well on other social platforms will help you uncover posts that deserve a spot in your boosted posts plan on Facebook.

We'll be covering evaluating and measuring your current content performance in greater depth when we talk about metrics and insights near the end of this book.

Facebook Lead Ads

These are quickly becoming my favorite ads and the one I'm willing to invest most heavily in. Conversely, they are the hardest to set up properly with more moving parts than the other types of ads.

These are similar to a standard News Feed ad, but clicking the *call to action* launches a native lead form on Facebook. Because it's a native Facebook form, it prefills things like Name and Email to save time (the user can still edit these fields). With such a pain-free form, the conversion rates are high, so cost per lead is often much lower and the results much more effective than using forms on your own website.

As Google has rolled out their AMP (Accelerated Mobile Page) specification, lead generating forms on your own website will see their performance chopped. The AMP spec doesn't even include forms, and it heralds a shift from favoring desktop users, to favoring mobile users.

It's easy to blame Google's unilateral decision to punish web forms for the impact this will have on our lead generating efforts, but the fact is the shift to mobile use is something that's been coming for a great while

It's this very thing that makes Facebook Lead ads so spectacular. Because Facebook has all the user's data, they can pre-populate the forms with a single click. With many sites now regularly see mobile visits in the 60% and above range compared to all visits, mobile users find it a pain to complete forms, you must find a way to reach customers on the device they are using and in a way that takes the least amount of effort to overcome even the smallest barrier to getting that lead submitted.

They are also the most highly traceable since they lead directly to conversions and when combined with offers can generate a lot of leads that go directly to the salespeople. Combined with custom audiences for retargeting website visitors to specific pages, they can be extremely effective. We've seen conversion rates of 15-18% for well-targeted audiences. Given that the average conversion rate for websites is less than 3%, I'd call that spectacular.

Studies have shown that as many as 70% or more of customers buy from the first dealer who contacts them. Why wait hours or even a day or two to get back to a customer that's just expressed a specific interest in your offer?

I've solved this problem by applying Zapier's new multi-step Zaps to the problem. Using this, I can have the Facebook Leads emailed to the store managers for distribution immediately as they come in. While this means the sales staff is slightly inconvenienced by having to manually enter the leads into our CRM, it also means they follow up within minutes of when the lead arrives.

Yes, you'll have to upgrade from the free account to the $15 basic account to use this process, but it's well worth it, and it's far cheaper than some of the other dealer services out there that do this. I'll go into detail on using Zapier right after we look at the process for creating the lead ads themselves.

For their lead ads, Facebook has built an advanced form editor which covers a wide range of form options, including a number of standard questions that can be asked with either text fields or a preset list in a dropdown select.

I recommend keeping the questions to a minimum, but throwing in a random question up front can help increase your conversion rate. That's because if we strip down the form to just the most basic five liner (First

Name, Last Name, Email Address, Phone Number, Zip Code), we end up asking only the most invasive questions. The ones that people are most reluctant to answer. So beginning the form with something like:

My #1 concern when buying a new vehicle is: Choose One — Safety, Reliability, Economy.

Because Facebook splits up the fields so they get no more than two questions at a time, users don't get hit with those highly invasive questions too early.

We use the zip code to confirm which rooftop the lead belongs to, all though for the purpose the lead ads we have created separate lead ads for each rooftop since each rooftop also has it's own page.

Just remember, shorter is better and less intrusive is better.

After they complete the form, you can include a *Visit Website* link. Treat a Lead Ad like any other customer journey, and make sure you send customers to a relevant page after they complete the form.

This is why an offer (for example a $25 gift card for completing an application in store) can be so powerful. You'll get a lot of people registering. Then you can take them to a landing page where they can download the $25 coupon to bring into the store with them. Count the coupons and divide by the clicks you've paid for and you've got your conversion rate. Add a website tracking pixel to the landing page and you can remarket these customers with a different campaign later.

Now that you know more about lead ads and their importance, let's see how to create your first lead ads campaign.

1. We're going back to the Power Editor so click *Download to Power Editor* at the top of the page. Select your ad account and hit *Download*;

2. Next, click *Create Campaign* and choose the *Lead Generation* objective for your campaign;

3. If it's not there, you can try to reset Power Editor – you can find the "Reset Power Editor" feature in the top right corner of the page, next to the "Help" button. And even if that doesn't help, you might need to wait for a few more weeks until it's released to all advertisers;

4. Next, navigate to the ad set level, create a new ad set and click *Edit*;

5. On the ad set level, you will be asked to choose your Facebook Page and accept the Terms of Services for lead ads;

6. As with any other campaigns, you will also need to specify the campaign settings: Budget, Schedule, Target Audience,

Placement, Optimization & Pricing, and Advanced Delivery;

7. If you set the budget to *Lifetime Budget*, instead of *Daily Budget* you'll have my favorite option available in the next section, so do that;

8. Overall I prefer to run ads on a scheduled *from* date and *to* date, but even more specifically I want the ads to only run when the store is open. In this way, the sales staff can respond quickly to leads coming in, rather than have leads sit overnight or from Saturday night till Monday morning. You can do this by choosing *More Options* under the schedule section;

9. Finally, in the Optimization & Pricing section, select if you want to bid for *Leads* or *Clicks*.

I recommend you bid for leads, since Facebook will use its own algorithms to optimize your campaigns by showing them to people that are more likely to convert. The later will focus on generating as many clicks as possible, including *like, share, comment, like page, see more* and other clicks. This will extend your reach and cost, but not necessarily generate more leads.

Once you're happy with all the settings, move to the ad level.

1. If you haven't already, click "Create Ad" and hit "Edit" to open

the editing window. You'll need to complete the usual fields for the ad creative: *Text, Headline, News Feed Link Description, Image* and *Call-to-Action*.

2. Avoid common Facebook ad mistakes, such as not customizing your text, and pushing features instead of benefits. Also make sure the ad is value-driven and has a clear call-to-action;

3. Now the most important part of your campaign – creating a new Lead Form. Click on *Create New Form* to open the lead form creation window;

4. Choose a name and a language for your lead generation form. Be sure to choose a descriptive name, not just Form 1 and Form2. This will almost certainly become a source of confusion.

5. Select what user information you want to collect from people who sign up. It can include: Contact Fields (First Name, Last Name, Phone number, Street address, City, State, Province, Country, Post code, Zip code), Demographic Questions (Date of birth, Gender, Marital status, Relationship status, Company name, Military status), and Work Information (Job title, Work phone number, Work email). Remember, shorter is better. Less intrusive is better. The purpose of the lead form isn't to make the salesman's job easier; it's to get the foot in the door with an email and phone number.

6. You can also add to three *Custom Questions* to your lead forms i
    you require specific information. Just click "Add Custom
    Question", enter the question headline and multiple choice
    answers, or leave it blank for open-ended questions. Another
    good way to use this is to include a, *What is your time frame for
    purchasing?* question with answers like less than 30 days, 30-60
    Days, etc ;

7. Once you're happy with the question and the information, click
    Next to add a link to your *Privacy Policy* and add any optional
    disclaimer.

*Don't have a privacy policy on your website? Then you're also losing some
search engine love from Google. Get one added to your site, ASAP. As far
as disclaimers go, you should probably add at least, "No cash value.
Restrictions may apply. See dealer for details," for any coupon or discount
We also add a consent to contact agreement to the form that allows us to
call, email and/or text them to follow-up.*

1. Review campaign settings in the ad set level and check your ad
    creative for any typos.
2. Finally, click on the big green button "Upload Changes" at the
    top of the page to send your campaign to your ad account.

Advertisers must not create Lead Ads Questions to certain types of information; primarily information that could be used to scam or discriminate against someone. Here are some other examples of no-no's for questions:

- Government-issued identifiers (such as social security numbers or driver's license numbers);

- Financial information and Account numbers (such as bank account numbers);

- Health information;

- Insurance information;

- Usernames or passwords;

- Race or ethnicity;

- Sexual orientation or information about the sexual life of the individual;

- Religion or philosophical beliefs;

- Political affiliation;

- Trade Union membership status; or

- Criminal or arrest history.

After you uploaded the changes, a new section of *"Ad Links"* will appear above the ad preview (still in the ads level in Power Editor). You can click on the link *View on Mobile*, which will send a notification to the Facebook app on your phone with an active link to your ad.

You can then see the ad on your mobile phone and go through the signup process by yourself, to make sure everything is working correctly:

Conventionally, to retrieve any leads your ad campaign generated, go to your Facebook page and click on *Publishing Tools*. Then click on *Forms Library* in the sidebar to see a list of all forms that you created, together with a number of leads it generated. This is where choosing good descriptive names helps avoid confusion. Click on 'Download' to begin the download process – you'll download a .csv file with all the leads and the additional information people filled in. All of this makes collecting leads a huge pain-in-the-behind. There are a number of startups that will do this for you, collecting your leads and posting them directly to your CRM. Most of them are expensive uni-taskers specifically designed to take advantage of the auto dealer community.

That's where Zapier comes in. Zapier has recently rolled out multi-step Zaps. One of the best uses of these is in combination with Facebook Lead Ads. When Facebook first announced lead ads, I was very excited. As mobile supplants desktop use, forms are becoming less and less effective as lead collecting elements of a website. Facebook Lead ads use forms, but with those forms Facebook uses information on file to simplify fill out the forms. The problem was that you had to keep going back to Facebook to collect the leads. This hardly makes keeping up with the leads a timely operation.

How I've handled that is by linking the Facebook Lead ads to a Gmail account through Zapier. So I get a Zap every time a new lead is submitted. It's an easy step-by-step process, linking your Facebook account and page, then building the email to be forwarded.

You can even set it up to forward to multiple emails. Here are the step to setting it up for yourself.

1. Create a new Zap and choose Facebook Lead ads as the Zap source.
2. Choose new lead as the trigger.
3. Connect your leads account.
4. Edit the Options and choose the page and form you want to connect to.
5. Now you're going to connect a separate step. Choose Send Email as the next Zap.
6. Connect to the Gmail account.
7. Choose edit template and build your email content. Be sure to include the lead content by choosing the content icon.
8. Test the Zap and enable it. Now whomever you decided to

email step 7 will be notified as leads come in and not whenever you can get around to downloading the file from your Facebook page.

As much as I love lead ads, there are a few drawbacks I should mention. First, they can be difficult to integrate with your CRM directly and will likely require at least some manual processing. It can be complicated to follow the lead from the initial sign up, to a thank you page, a sales page, or an upsell page.

Secondly, and maybe most important, lead ads make remarketing more complicated. When you send traffic to a traditional landing page, not only can you get new leads, but you can also use the Facebook website tracking pixel to capture those that didn't sign up and re-engage them with other offers. This becomes more difficult with the Lead Ads campaigns.

Using Video

The importance of video on Facebook cannot be overstated. Facebook and YouTube (Google) are involved in an arms race of sorts, and video is at the heart of it. Facebook gives you preference of placement for videos done correctly, and YouTube is Google. Google loves Google's stuff, so you can bet that outside of Facebook, YouTube videos will help you

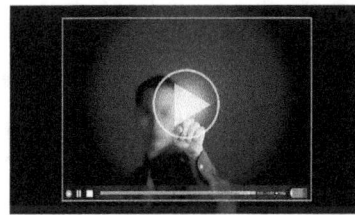

perform better when embedded on your vehicle's pages or in your blog.

Images generate about five times the level of engagement as text status updates, but video generates fifteen times that level of engagement. It is simply the best way to maximize your reach and your ad dollars.

Native video

A video posted specifically on Facebook and not a link from a different platform is referred to as *Native Content*, as opposed to *linked* or *embedded content*. Native video often gets higher organic reach than videos that are hosted elsewhere because the videos automatically start to play as the user scrolls through their timeline, versus taking a click-action to engage. I know that simple click doesn't seem like it should be much of a hurdle to overcome, but it genuinely is. Once our eye sees that movement we are immediately attracted to it. Not only will the video get more views, but also it'll get higher play-through rates. The first: 15-seconds of almost any video will get viewed by 95% of users, but by the end of the first minute viewership can drop to as low as 5%. By using captions, keeping the video short and making it as engaging as possible we've seen play-through rates double or even triple of other dealership videos.

Because native video starts playing in a Facebook user's' newsfeed as they scroll over it, to be successful creating this type of content, you need to grab your user's attention right away. To do this, try these tips:

- Make it interesting enough to be engaging with or without sound or at least have captions included (more on that in a moment).
- Make a statement with your first few frames—you need to get your viewer to stick around.
- Use smart copy—the text that you post with your video will help create interest, curiosity and set the stage for your video for your audience.

Shooting A Good Walk-Around Video

So this might seem like a radical shift in gears, but it isn't. Walk-around videos have proven themselves to be one of the best Facebook tools for generating interest available. I'm going to break this section into three pieces; shooting a good video, what to do with the video once you've got it, and how to use it on Facebook.

Here are the steps to making a good walk-around video:

1. Pull the car out and position it so the background isn't overly busy. If you can get your streetside sig in the frame that perfect. Introduce yourself, the dealership and the vehicle, "Hi this is Cliff VanMeter from Cliff's Autoland and I'd like to show you this 2004 Toyota Rav 4."

2. You have two ways to shoot, Have someone else hold the camera (phone), or shoot selfie style. I personally recommend selfie style. Show your face on screen to start, then pan across to the vehicle.

3. Start with a 3/4 view establishing shot from the front of the vehicle and walk around SLOWLY highlighting any special features. For example, on a minivan this might be dual side doors, on a truck or SUV the tow package or 4x4. Alloy wheels, special paint, etc. It's okay to get your hands into the video, in fact it's good to see you touching stuff and pointing. Your hands act as a surrogate for the viewer.

4. Show the engine and talk about your warranties, inspections and guarantees.

5. Show the interior and highlight any special features like third-

row seats. Turn on the radio, honk the horn, and show the console. For SUVs and minivans, open the back and show the interior from there as well. Again, highlight special features such as power adapters in the back, entertainment centers, or the flip-up seats.

6. Show your face again, and finish up with, "This has been Cliff VanMeter from Cliff's Auto Land with our newly arrived 2004 Toyota Rav4 with automatic 4x4. To see this vehicle or any of the 100s of vehicles we offer, give me a call at ###-###- #### ext.###."

7. Upload the video to YouTube -- I know this is a book about Facebook, but we'll get to that in a second.. Make the name of the video, "Yr. Make Model - Store" (for example, "2004 Toyota Rav4 4x4 - Cliff's Auto Land Kalamazoo"). Include your name and the company/store name in the description, "Clifford VanMeter from Cliff's Auto Land in Kalamazoo, MI shows off a newly arrived 2004 Toyota Rav4 4x4 in this short walk-around video." You can even be a little whimsical., "Here's Cliff from Cliff's Auto Land in Kalamazoo with the *Cliff Notes* on this great Toyota RAV4 with automatic four wheel drive."

Here are a few *don'ts*:

- Don't show dings or dents, rust spots, etc.
- Don't show dirt under or between the seats.
- Don't leave the white paper floor mats in or any kind of trash for that matter.
- Don't talk mileage or price.
- Don't linger on the dash long enough to read the mileage.
- Don't shoot cars with dirt or snow on them.

A couple more general tips: good audio is more important than good video. Keep the camera close to the speaker for the best audio. Also avoid shooting on windy days, or by noisy roadsides. Move the vehicle somewhere sheltered or quieter. People will not sit through bad audio, no matter how attractive the vehicle or presentation.

Three things affect the effectiveness (viewership) of your video:

1. Market size. Obviously if you're in a market like Chicago, your potential viewership shoots up dramatically.
2. Vehicle Choice. Depending on the time of year and gas prices, people will choose to sit through a video on the kind of vehicles they are most interested in buying. This is not necessarily the kind of vehicles you sell the most of. For example, if you're selling Chevy Impalas hand-over-fist,

shooting a lot of Chevy Impala videos might still not be the best strategy. You need to capture their attention. Jeeps, Full Sized SUV, and compact cars (especially when gas prices are high) are always good bets. In northern climes, 4x4s, and all-wheel drive vehicles are going to generate the most interest. You're looking for click-bait.

3. Presenter and Presentation. The presenter and presentation have a lot to do with it. Attractive people have an advantage. Female sales staff also have an advantage, as studies have shown that most women would rather hear a woman speak, and so would most men. Good sound, good clear video, use of humor, etc. All these things affect the viewership.

One thing you don't need is a professional spokesperson, or even professionally shot video. Almost all smart phone now shoot HD video and frankly, the less you make the video have the slickly produced look of a commercial and the more conversational and relaxed you make it sound, the better. I'm not saying unprofessional, I'm saying casually professional. People aren't looking to be sold to from their newsfeed; they want to be talked to.

There are reasons we upload to YouTube first, including YouTube's excellent captioning and shake removal capabilities. There are lots of tutorials on uploading to YouTube. So instead I'm going to concentrate on the captioning features and how to use them.

The best way to caption the video is using YouTube's CC tools.

1. Select CC from the toolbar above the video.

2. Choose your language.

3. Select Transcribe and auto-sync from the options menu.

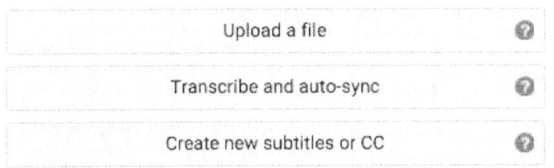

This option allows you to type as the speaker talks, when you stop typing the video plays, but it pauses as you type to let you catch up. Very nice feature. It automatically syncs the captions to the video when you hit set timings.

4. Wait till the timing are complete and choose Publish. Once you've published the captions, go to the *Actions* menu and download an .srt file.

5. Last step is to go to Creator Studio (under your account on the top right). Once there go to the video manager and choose download mp4 from the *Actions* menu next to *Edit* below the date. You've now downloaded the cleaned up video from YouTube.

Why is captioning so important? Why upload to YouTube just to download and upload to Facebook? Facebook videos auto-play in the timeline, but without sound till you click on them. Sure you could embed a video from YouTube, but it wouldn't auto-play and that reduces views. Captioning is critical because about 30% of the people who see the video in their timeline don't click on it to play the sound. They just watch with the captions. Using both auto-play and captions, you'll get a bigger audience to watch the video all the way through. We' see shortly why that's important.

Go to your Facebook page and choose upload photo/video. While that's processing, go to your saved captions file and rename it like this -- filename.en_US.srt. For example: 2011kiasoul.en_US.srt. It has to be in this format. Then choose the captions tab and select Upload SRT File.

You're not done yet. Now choose *Add Button*. I like to add the *Shop Now* or *Learn More* button. This puts a live link to a page on your website at the end of the video. This is why we are so concerned with increasing the play-through rate. This button only appears at the end of the video. If you're viewers aren't sticking around, they don't get the link. Of

Contact Jessica

Fill out th
Don't for
your tim

Name *

First

Hi, I'm Jessica. Thanks for watching my video. This is just an example of the kind of the great cars we have. Every one comes with a FREE 36-Month/36,000 Mile warranty. Whether you're interested in the vehicle you just saw, or one similar, I can help. We literally have hundreds of vehicles to choose from.

Phone *

Best Tim

Select (

Sub

course you can, and should, include a link in the description, but this is far less likely to generate clickthroughs than the *Shop Now* button.

This button is a huge traffic generator, especially when combined with a special landing page for the salesperson in the video.

I use a distraction free contact page that includes a script to detect for mobile and presents a click-to-call button right on the landing page that links to their direct dial phone number and extension where necessary. Here's what that script looks like:

Call Me at ###-###-####<a href="tel:###-###-####"><img class="alignnone wp-image-114183 size-full aligncenter" src="https://website.com/wp-

content/uploads/2015/08/call-me.png" alt="call-me" width="422" height="114" /></a>

This hides the button on desktops and tablets where it shows the phone and extension as text, but puts it front and center on mobile phones.

Creating these landing pages can be a lot of work, especially for larger operations, but they also get you a lot more buy-in from the sales staff. After all, every lead they generate from their video goes right in their pocket.

After uploading the video to Facebook, you've still got YouTube embed for your website, where Google will give you extra SEO love for having a YouTube video. Now it's time to boost that video post for even more exposure.

Analytics

To effectively determine which actions you should be pursuing on Facebook, you must first how to measure your success when using Facebook ads and actions.

One of the best things about online advertising is the ability to measure everything; compare everything. The more you know about how effective your ads are, the better you'll be about predicting which kinds of ads to run in the future.

In this section, we'll outline your journey from your campaign's first post to that sweet moment of ROI. When you use the most relevant metrics you're bound to get the best results.

You'll get a good idea of your effectiveness by picture by keeping an eye on:

- The number of Page Likes added;
- The number of actions taken (engagements - likes, comments and shares);
- The number of unique individuals who engaged with your brand;
- The number of click-throughs on your links;
- The number of unique individuals who saw your posts;

- The number of potential times those people could have seen your posts;
- Your overall engagement rate.

You can reach a huge number of people when your target audience and other influencers engage. This spreads your content and increases your brand awareness. Great content leads to more engagement. From there you get increased reach as more fans opt-in, adding fuel to the machine.

These calculations may seem complicated, but they are critical to understanding the level of engagement you're getting from your audience. Without that you'll never be able to determine the most cost-effective methods for targeting and engaging your audiences. Conversations lead to conversions, remember?

So for the next few pages I'm going to break down each component that plays an active role in your brand's Facebook success. Most of these will be comparisons, No number exists in a vacuum.

Page Likes

It's important to understand the distinction between page likes, and post likes. Page likes indicate the size of the community you're building on Facebook. Post likes, on the other hand, are specific to a status update, photo or video.

A growing audience on Facebook is the sign of a healthy community. You need to do more than measure your new Page Likes to understand

how your audience is growing to identify effective tactics for sustaining growth. Determine how users are finding your Page by analyzing your Like Sources.

Like Sources can be found within Facebook Insights. Like Sources within the Facebook Insights tool are broken out into five segments:

1. Ads
2. On Your Page
3. Your Posts
4. Uncategorized Mobile
5. Others

Within the Facebook Insights data export, Like Sources can be segmented even further. Dozens of sources exist; but only the sources your Page was liked from will appear in your data export.

Facebook provides a description for some of the most common Like Sources in its Insights developer documentation:

- **Page Suggestion** — People who liked you page through the invite of an admin;

- **Timeline** — People who liked you page from the Likes section of their own timeline or someone else's;

- **Registration** — People you added as admins;

- **Mobile** — People who liked you page from a mobile device;

- **Wizard-Suggestion** — People who liked you page in the New User Wizard when registering for Facebook;

- **Profile-Connect** — People who liked your page on the page itself or in a news feed or ticker story.

This list gives you a good idea of how in-depth you can get and how much you can learn about your company's Facebook presence.

Like Sources can help you understand how users are discovering and liking your Page. They also provide context for how your other digital marketing efforts relates to increases in Likes on your page. Here are some of the questions Like Sources help you answer.

- Are external connects such as clicks on social plugins from your website doing a good job driving users to your Facebook Page?

- When you do more to integrate social plugins, do you see more Likes? This is a great place for A/B testing. For example, test positioning. Put your Facebook Like button on the top of your website for one month then move it to the bottom for the following month to learn. Watch Page Likes and you'll quickly see which works better.

- What percentage of new Likes is being driven by Facebook Ads? Comparing thiss percentage to similar metrics from other social networks will help you understand the resources you need to devote to Facebook compared to other networks.

- If you are using a third-party app such as a contest or poll, how well is it contributing to fan growth? Facebook Insights are a very good tool for comparing third-party apps to find out which is most effective.

- How many users liked your Page from a mobile device, such as a smartphone or tablet? If a large audience liked your page from mobile, you'll want to spend some time making sure your content is optimized for mobile.

These are questions you can answer with data from Like Sources. From there, you can make more informed decisions about which tactics can be most effective in growing your page.

Paid vs. Unpaid Likes

Facebook advertising is a must for modern marketers, with most brands devoting at least a portion of their social media budget to advertising on the network.

It's important to be able to segment social media performance by paid vs. organic so that you can see how these activities complement one another. Organic engagement will always lag far behind paid engagement, so you should think of organic engagement like the gravy on the biscuits.

Likes are counted as paid when they occur within one day of viewing your ad or 28 days of clicking your ad.

Engagement

Engagement is the umbrella term we use for likes, comments and shares of your posts. There are several different reasons to pursue engagement:

- Drive traffic to your website for increased conversions;
- Building brand awareness and overall market penetration
- Increasing your Facebook likes and influence

Checking your engagement is the best way to get an overview of how you're doing; conduct content and competitive analyses; and set KPIs to determine the success of your campaigns.

Engagement on Facebook is just how we term all the different ways your social audience can interact with your posts. Engagement is what makes your posts show up in their and their friends Newsfeeds. It is a measure people's interest in your content and how willing they are to promote your content their circles of influence.

Facebook offers a huge number of options by which people can engage with your content. Sharing, commenting, liking, or clicking through are just some of the ways. This is what makes Facebook such a powerful, versatile platform for companies like yours. Using Facebook as the centerpiece of a conversation marketing plan, you can create brand advocates for your company, who will provide feedback, purchase products, and help you better understand your customers.

Understanding how well you interact with users on Facebook is a vital step towards developing successful marketing campaigns. Engagement is the total of several components during a specific period:

- Likes: When a user likes a brand post on your page;

- Comments: When a user comments on your brand post;

- Shares: When a user shares one of your posts with their friends.

Engagement is what spreads your content. You've probably heard the term, *going viral*. It's this organic spreading of content that mimics word-of-mouth; widely regarded as the best kind of advertising. Think of engagement as word-of-mouth on steroids.

The amount of engagement your posts receive can help you understand:

- Your content's ability to capture user attention;

- Your content's ability to compel user action

- The number of people who were served your post;

- Your brand visibility, because the engagement metric is a major factor in Facebook's News Feed algorithm, which determines the News Feeds your posts are displayed in and, ultimately, how many users that you're able to reach.

Facebook provides you with many sources of great data. The key is to learn to convert this data into information. Data is useful, but information is actionable. Finding operation data that you can use to influence operational decisions is the goal of all this.

One of my favorite bits of data is in the form of the People Engagement metric. It's a key Facebook measurement for discovering how many unique visitors are actively engaging with (liking, commenting, sharing, or clicking) on your Page.

The People Engaged or Engaged Users metric are shown in Facebook Insights on both the Overview and People tabs. People Engaged isn't just limited to the people who like your Page: anyone who engages with your Page is tallied in this count.

The Overview tab in Facebook Insights shows you how many people engaged with your posts, and how that number has gone changed in the last week. By looking at your progress over a longer period of time such as month-over-month or quarter-over- quarter, you'll get even more context as to how your results are aligning with your larger goals.

The People tab is where you can see the demographic breakdown of people who like your Page. The demographic information includes a gender, age, geographic, and language breakdown. This is great for helping determine how closely the audience matches your customer profile.

Measuring the number of people who engage with your brand goes beyond your Page's Like count. We want to know how many people are interacting with your Page. In other words, of all the people you were able to reach, these are the users who took action.

By monitoring the number of engaged users as a percentage of your audience, you'll determine whether you're growing an active or a passive audience.

The questions you need to answer are:

1. How active is your audience;
2. How good is your content is at driving action.

As we've talked about earlier in the book, your fans' engagement with your posts directly impacts your ability to reach your audience. If you can't engage users, they won't see your content and neither will their friends.

Reach & Impressions

One of our greatest concerns as marketers using Facebook is the number of people who are seeing our content. This is especially true when we're spending money to boost posts. This is where reach comes in. It's where the rubber hits the road.

Reach tells us how many people could have seen our content. It's a powerful performance indicator that shows us how well our social media strategy is working.

There are two types of reach: organic and paid. Understanding and measuring each tells you how and why your audience changes over time.

> Organic Reach: The number of unique people who saw your content in their News Feeds, tickers (where you see the latest

news show up in real time on the right-hand side of your newsfeed), or on your Page.

Paid Reach: The number of unique people who saw your paid content.

Measuring reach by type can help you pinpoint the factors that contributed to content views. If organic reach increased, it might be the result of more Likes on your Page or a particularly engaging post.

Monitoring paid reach and comparing it to organic reach tells you whether any changes were due to ads or organic activity. This quickly tells you where to put your money.

Reach also tells you how big your brand's effective audience is. It can be a more accurate measure of your Facebook audience than Page Likes, since not all the people who like your Page see your posts and many users who do see your posts do not Like your Page.

Facebook Reactions

Facebook Reactions quickly became a hot button issue when they debuted earlier this year. In theory they replace or complement the one-size-fits-all, "Like," button. Like most things that change on the web, some people loved them and some hated them. While Reactions may not change the overall way we market, but they do give people using

Facebook the opportunity to display a more diverse range of emotions. And that's a good thing? So now, in addition to Like, we have Love, Laughing (HaHa), Yay, Wow, Sad and Angry.

Facebook video has become a powerful content type for conversation marketers. Publishing native videos on Facebook has two main benefits:

- Native videos start playing immediately as people scroll through their Feed. Videos initially play silently, but people can tap the video to play it with sound in full screen. This is why the addition of captions is so important.

- Public videos from people and Pages will now show view counts to help people discover them.

Facebook serves up eight billion video views per day, which is double the amount that video content users were consuming in early 2015. Facebook's announced plans for video are a shot across the bow of YouTube and offer a fantastic opportunity for marketers.

Video has already become a critical part of our content mix. So it's important to understand the video-specific metrics that can help you measure and optimize your video content. Marketers now have access to engagement data for Facebook videos that goes beyond Likes, comments, and shares. These engagement metrics give is important signals for the success of our video content.

Video Views

When analyzing any content type, it's good to start broad and narrow your scope. Facebook only counts a view after the user has watched at least three seconds of a video.

So benchmarking total views can be a better measurement of your company's penetration among Facebook fans.

I know I've mentioned it before, but the most important take-away is that Facebook auto-plays native videos when a user scrolls through their feed, both on mobile and desktop. Because of the three-second delay, auto-play views demonstrate your ability to stop people and capture their attention.

	NATIVE VIDEOS	3RD PARTY VIDEOS	DIFFERENCE	RATIO
👍 LIKE	814	342	472	2x
↪ SHARE	168	63	105	3x
💬 COMMENTS	104	14	90	7x
👥 PEOPLE REACHED	181760	88950	92810	2x

As you can see by the table above, virtually every important metric improves with Facebook native videos when compared to third party embedded videos like YouTube. Not by any small margin either, but by as much as a factor of 700%.

While auto-play views speak to the impact of your video's intro to capture attention, click-to-play stats can demonstrate the quality of your caption, video title, and chosen still. To optimize your viewership, you'll want to watch these stats carefully and adjust your content accordingly.

Monitoring click-to-play rates over time will also give you a how well your videos are doing with your target audience. If more people are actively clicking to play your clips, they're demonstrating that your video is worth their time.

Views Between 3-30 Seconds

Focusing on views that ended before the 30-second mark gives you insight into which content that isn't engaging your audience. They started to watch your video, they made that initial commitment, then you lost them. The key then become to find out what went wrong?

Views that last longer than 30 seconds can be just as valuable. By analyzing which content has the most impact and retain viewers for the longest, you know which characteristics to focus on when developing new content.

Facebook Live Videos are in a special category of their own. Live Videos are real-time video posts on Facebook. You can subscribe to feeds to get notified the next time that person starts a live broadcast. Some stats you should know about:

- People spend 3x longer watching live video compared to a video that's pre-recorded

- Facebook Product Manager Vibhi Kant noted, "We're making a small update to News Feed so that Facebook Live videos are more likely to appear higher in News Feed when those videos are actually live, compared to after they are no longer live."

- Facebook's app preference to live video

As of now, there are no separate ways to measure Facebook Live Videos, other than the ones outlined above. So determining how well you are doing on Facebook Live is a bit more difficult. The feature does give you the advantage of being able to respond to comments from fans in real-time and mine future content using this enhanced engagement.

Understanding Your Facebook Audiences

There is more to understanding your audience on Facebook than just tracking page likes. Your likes might grow, for example, thanks to a special offer or promotion. That doesn't mean all those likes come from your target audience.

You need to dig deeper to develop the insights you need to create audience growth and maximize engagement. Audience analysis is about understanding the following:

- Who you're connecting with;

- Which type of content resonates with them;

- How you can more effectively build a community around your brand.

Here are some tactics that will get you focused on measuring the right things to help you interpret your Facebook audience analysis.

1. Measure the Audience You Actually Reach.

The Facebook users who see status updates, links, pictures and videos from your page aren't limited to the people who like your Page. Reach measures the unique number of people who saw your content. Tracking your increases and decreases in reach over time will help you understand how sharing your content affects your ability to expand and engage an audience.

As I've mentioned before, reach basically breaks down into two categories, or segments; organic and paid.

Organic reach is what you got because people liked, commented and and shared your content on their own. It's the engagement you generated because you were good, original, interesting or funny.

Paid reach is what you spent money on through advertising such as boosting posts. These are the engagements you bought.

By digging deeper into the analytics and insights for a specific time-frame, you'll be able to identify the exact content or campaigns that motivated your audiences to take action, either positively or negatively.

For instance, if you charted your brand's activity between 01/01/16 – 01/07/16 and there was a clear spike in activity, you could look back at what you did during that time period to determine the root cause of that spike.

2. Analyze Your Engaged Audience

The key to building your online presence and creating engagement with you audience is growing your audience over time. As your total number of Page Likes increases, you want to also grow the number of users who engage with your content. Seeing likes grow without increasing the number of engaged users means engagement, as a percent of users, is decreasing. That's not good. If anything you want to see engaged.

The fact is, users who like you page often don't ever actually come back to your page. They get their views of your content through their news feed. So Page Likes are really just a kind of permission to converse. If your users increase but the percentage of engaged users doesn't, the value of that audience growth is negligible.

When compared against your posts during a given time period, the percentage of audience engaging tells you what types of content are driving real value from the social audience you've built.

3. Create Contexts for Like Growth

Your total Page Likes isn't the only metric you should be paying attention to, but Like growth will serve as an indicator of your Facebook community's health. Putting your Page Likes in proper context will also help you identify tactics to increase your audience size.

Here's how:

- *Look at Your Like Sources.* By analyzing where your Likes are coming from, you can determine where Facebook users were, what device they were using, and properly segment paid sources such as ads or and organic sources such as shares. You can also identify which content (paid or organic) was most successful at generating likes, then focus your attention on creating more content of that type.

- ***Compare with Other User Actions.*** By looking at Likes, comments, shares, and clicks for a given time period, you can easily see which other kinds of activities Likes aligned with. Similar to using Google Analytics to determine what other ads people clicking on your ads also clicked. This gives you insights into what your community is interested in besides your content. Applying that information allows you to create relevant content within their zones of interests, potentially increasing their engagement.

- ***Check Out Your Page and Tab Visits.*** Information from your Visits tab will tell you which parts of your Page are major attractions for people who just Liked you and people who are still deciding whether they should Like you. Just compare the number of times your Page tabs generated views alongside Page Likes created during a given time period.

- ***Consider Your External Referrers.*** Examine your progress over time in context with the number of people visiting your

Page from off Facebook sites such as other social media sites
(like Twitter or Instagram). By carefully studying this data, you
can determine which off Facebook sites are delivering the most
traffic and growing your community. Despite my focus here on
Facebook only, you might find one of those external sources
worth investigating as a possible secondary promotional source.

Identify Who Likes Your Page

When I talk about identifying who likes your brand, I'm not talking
about identifying individual users, but identifying what your users base
looks like. Understanding that they have in common. You can do this by
establishing an audience baseline using Facebook Insights demographic
data.

For example, understanding where your fans are located can help you
decide about what kind of content you share and when you publish it.
Adding content relating to current and upcoming local events is a great
way to generate shares, comments and likes. We call this Newsjacking,
and it's a great way to generate content around current events.

I've mentioned before that I currently reside in Kalamazoo, Michigan.
Kalamazoo just happens to be exactly halfway between Detroit and
Chicago. If I wanted to use sports to create a little controversy and
generate comments, I could use that as a newsjacking opportunity to

drive fan engagement by comparing the Chicago Cubs to the Detroit Tigers.

Things like upcoming festivals and fairs can also be newsjacking opportunities; major area concert announcements, area conventions or events etc. It all has to do with pinpointing your users' interests and playing to those.

Another important factor is to determine the age range and sex of your target audience. Obviously different products are going to be aimed at different ages. The same is true for males and females. Whether you've got a big Chevy Silverado 4x4 to promote, a cute little PT Cruiser, you need to be aware of the correct audience focus for that.

Once you've established a baseline, you can dig deeper into your demographics by adjusting your buyer personas so you map certain products and content topics to specific personas. Then track engagemen with content that ties back to personas as one of your regular audience metrics. Over time you'll be able to dial in your content to activate your most engaged audiences.

One last thing to track and analyze. Timing is everything, so by comparing how your Page Likes align with the time of day your fans are online, you'll be able to time your posts to optimize Page Likes.

How to Measure the Impact of Visual Content

Visual content has by far the greatest impact when it comes to driving engagement. But with so many services for creating and distributing images, and so many types of visual content, including memes, photos, and videos, how can you tell which work and which don't? The only way is to analyze your visual content as aggressively as any other content and create a strategy based on previous successes.

With Facebook Insights, you can see how many photos were viewed, videos were watched, and links were clicked over a specific period of time. Then use your audience profiles to compare what they are most attracted to. Should you be devoting resources to putting together videos or are photos more appealing to your audience?

Also measure engagement types overall against per-post engagement on your various content types. For example, you might see a spike in engagement on photos, but you also post more photos than any videos. It's important to make sure you're comparing apples to apples. By breaking down how successful your photos are on a per-post basis; looking at Likes, comments, and shares you'll discover how valuable the engagement you're getting is.

Remember, comments are best for triggering both further engagement and Facebook's own algorithms for how much News Feed love you're going to get. More comments will increase the frequency with which you show up in your fans' feeds. The next most important type of engagement are shares, since shares push your content out to the connections of your fans. Likes are still important, but do the least to help you increase your organic reach. You need to apply a scoring approach to how you classify the importance of the engagement.

Build Video Content Using Insights

In their race against Google and YouTube, Facebook is putting an increasing emphasis in users feeds. You'll see greatly increased engagement on native videos compared to other media types

So videos are clearly seeing more organic reach than photos, but as we've seen, producing high-quality and relevant videos is a much more complex and time consuming task than producing and posting photos. This makes many marketers reluctant to focus their efforts on properly posting video.

Everything you do regarding the production of the videos you post should be optimized to produce the maximum benefit possible. This is where your analysis of your video insights will help you focus on creating the best and most engaging videos possible.

Understanding how long users are viewing your content is a critical measurement. Sure, the standard rule of thumb is two minutes or less, but understanding YOUR optimal viewing length is going to work in your favor to get you that maximum viewership.

Facebook Insights will give you this information allows you to identify the optimal viewing length before users tune out. Then it becomes a training issue for the staff who are creating the videos. Earlier when I was talking about walk-around videos, for example, we know for that client that 95% of viewers watch the first 15-seconds of the video. We have optimized the videos so that more than 20% of viewers are still watching by the end of the video. Obviously our goal is to get that even percentage even higher, but 20% is huge compared to the 5% many videos have watching at that point.

The road to this increase took us directly through the Insights. We discovered that the most watched videos shared traits such as:

- Female presenters;

- Good sound with few audio background distractions like wind noise;

- Selfie style as opposed to shot by a third person;

- Engagement by the presenter, things like getting their hands into the shot and touching the vehicle.

Pretty much the same advice I gave you earlier in this book. So how does this relate to what you should be doing? It gives you a place to start, but analyzing your insights as you go will be what makes your audience focus complete.

In addition, when looking at a specific video, you should be able to identify specific retention loses. This way you can discover which areas of your content need the most attention. For example, if you identify that your loose 50% of viewers at the 14-second mark, you can focus on that part of your video to discover what might have caused people to bounce. So this helps inform your content development if you ensure your analysis and testing are done properly.

Time to Call in SWOT

If you've never heard of or used the SWOT technique in your analysis process, you've been missing an opportunity. SWOT analysis is widely regarded as one of the best ways to develop a consolidated strategic approach to your brand message.

Simply put, SWOT looks at your brand's *Strengths, Weaknesses, Opportunities,* and *Threats* at the current time.

It is a common marketing practice you should be aware of. By asking these questions, you bring the insights you've gained into your planning process to contribute to your overall social strategy.

- **Strengths**: We're not looking at your brand's overall market strengths, we're looking at the strengths of your Facebook presence. Those things that give you an advantage over competitors on social media. Where are you being proactive? Where are you exceptional?

- **Weaknesses**: Where are you weak? What are you doing or not doing that put you at a disadvantage to competitors. When you look at your industry benchmarks, are you failing to meet those standards? What are you failing to achieve?

- **Opportunities**: If you look closely enough, you'll find where your competitor's social media strategies are weak. What are some things your competitors could be doing better? Strategies that you could co opt an improve on? Apart from your competitors, where are you still weak on social media? Which o Facebook's marketing capabilities are you not taking full advantage of?

- **Threats**: What aspects of social media are impacting your quality, reputation, uniqueness, and the overall value of your social presence. Where is your company at risk? Where should you be devoting resources immediately?

In Conclusion

We've touched on a lot of techniques in this book and if you only take away one thing make it this: ***Everything connects.***

That's why they call it a web. You profile affects your page, your page is affected by advertising and promotions both off and online.

Each of these might at first seem like a discrete element of your marketing plan, but I assure you they are not. They are all cogs in your marketing machine.

To paraphrase Henry Ford, "The man that stops *talking to his customers* to save money, is like the man that stops a clock to save time."

So whether you're just getting the conversation started, or you're already in it, do as much as you can, as often as you can, and you'll see measurable, repeatable results.

Online & Dealership Acronyms

Every industry has its own language. The online world is filled with acronyms. As much as I've tried to make this book relatively jargon-free, it's good to understand what these mean.

You're sure to encounter most or all of these in the course of mastering online marketing.

SRP – Search Results Page: A dynamically created webpage that shows the vehicle results of a specific search query on a car dealer's website.

VRP – Vehicle Results Page: Same as SRP, depending on the company some may use VRP in place of SRP

VLP – Vehicle Listings Page: This is generally a listing of available inventory on the dealer's website. This will be distinct from VDPs because it will list a number of vehicles. Depending on the company some may use VLP in place of SRP.

VDP – Vehicle Details Page: A page on an automotive retail website that represents a single, specific vehicle. This is where a consumer finds all the information related to a vehicle.

UX – User Experience: A term that's meant to subjectively quantify what a consumer's experience might be using a website. A good UX is one that's easy to navigate, is mobile responsive and anticipates the consumers needs.

ADF – Auto-lead Data Format: An XML based standard for taking customer information submitted via a form on your or a 3rd party website and inputting it directly into your CRM.

BDC – Business Development Center: A department within a dealership that's tasked with driving and retaining traffic for the sales and/or service teams of the store. There are various ways to staff a BDC, but in general the personnel handle some or all of the inbound phone calls, Internet leads, unsold follow up & retention activities.

CRM – Customer Relationship Management: Typically a cloud based app or program, a CRM gives a dealership's sales team a way to track, manage and follow up with each customer that submits a lead, call the dealership and/or walks through the door.

DMS – Dealer Management System: A software system used to manage the operations of all departments within a dealership. Modules within the DMS exist for sales, finance, service, parts and administration. Vehicle inventory data feeds are also parsed through the DMS.

GA – Google Analytics: The free analytics suite that you'll find installed on the vast majority of car dealership websites.

PIT — Precise Interest Targeting. For Facebook this kind of precision targeting is generally accomplished using custom audiences or lookalike audiences. These audiences target a specific subset of Facebook users who are more likely to be receptive to your ad.

UV – Unique Visitors: Now known simply as, "Users," within Google Analytics, this is the number of individual people who visit a website

BR – Bounce Rate: Expressed as a percentage, bounce rate is a function that occurs when a user navigates away from a website after viewing only one page.

TOS – Time on Site: Also known as Session Duration in Google Analytics, this is the average amount of time in minutes and seconds a user spends on a website in a single visit. More time on the site generally leads to higher conversions.

SERP – Search Engine Results Page: The list of results a search engine displays after a user enters a search query.

SEO – Search Engine Optimization: A set of strategies and tactics implemented on a website to gain visitors by achieving a higher organic ranking on search engine result pages.

SEM – Search Engine Marketing: The process of driving web traffic by purchasing text ads on search engines such as Google and Bing. SEM is often referred to in general as Paid Search.

CPC – Cost Per Click: The measurement of the cost per click for campaigns based on impressions.

PPC – Pay Per Click: The measurement of campaigns where you only pay if a user clicks. Paid search is the most relevant example of PPC – while your ad may show up in a SERP, you only pay your ad is clicked.

CTR – Click Through Rate: This measures the percentage of clicks per impressions an ad receives.

CPM – Cost Per Thousand: No that's not a typo, the M in CPM stands for mile which is Latin for thousand. A common measurement used across digital and traditional advertising that refers to the price a network charges for one thousand ad impressions.

eCPM – Effective Cost Per Mile: This metric accounts for over or under delivery of an impressions based campaign. Campaigns that over delivered will give you an eCPM lower than the CPM you actually paid and a campaign that under delivers impressions will give you an eCPM higher than what you actually paid.

KPI – Key Performance Indicator: Is a metric or group of metrics a dealership will use to determine performance in specific areas of operations. You might have KPI's for your website, SEO, customer retention and so on.

ROI – Return on Investment: I would think everyone would know this one, but just incase...ROI is the profit earned from a specific advertising campaign.

GTM – Google Tag Manager: A free tool that makes it easy for marketers to setup and manage conversion tracking, site analytics, remarketing and other tags on your website.

SMM — Social Media Marketing: Basically what this book is about. Strategies and tactics to optimize your social media campaigns to deliver high conversions rates and great ROI.

www.ingramcontent.com/pod-product-compliance
Lightning Source LLC
Chambersburg PA
CBHW070249190526
45169CB00001B/348